W9-ABV-826

INTRODUCING
ISSUES WITH
OPPOSING
VIEWPOINTS®

The Electoral College and the Popular Vote

Lisa Idzikowski, Book Editor

GREENHAVEN
PUBLISHING

Published in 2018 by Greenhaven Publishing, LLC
353 3rd Avenue, Suite 255, New York, NY 10010

Copyright © 2018 by Greenhaven Publishing, LLC

First Edition

All rights reserved. No part of this book may be reproduced in any form without permission in writing from the publisher, except by a reviewer.

Articles in Greenhaven Publishing anthologies are often edited for length to meet page requirements. In addition, original titles of these works are changed to clearly present the main thesis and to explicitly indicate the author's opinion. Every effort is made to ensure that Greenhaven Publishing accurately reflects the original intent of the authors. Every effort has been made to trace the owners of the copyrighted material.

Library of Congress Cataloging-in-Publication Data

Names: Idzikowski, Lisa, editor.
Title: The Electoral College and the popular vote / Lisa Idzikowski, book
  editor.
Description: New York : Greenhaven Publishing, 2018. | Series: Introducing
  issues with opposing viewpoints | Includes bibliographical references and
  index. | Audience: Grade 9 to 12.
Identifiers: LCCN 2017039270 | ISBN 9781534501935 (library bound) | 9781534502741
  (paperback)
Subjects: LCSH: Electoral college—United States—Juvenile literature. |
  Presidents—United States—Election—Juvenile literature. |
  Elections—United States. | Voting—United States—Juvenile literature.
Classification: LCC JK529 .E46 2018 | DDC 324.6/3—dc23
LC record available at https://lccn.loc.gov/2017039270

Manufactured in the United States of America

Website: http://greenhavenpublishing.com

Contents

Foreword

Indulging in a wide spectrum of ideas, beliefs, and perspectives is a critical cornerstone of democracy. After all, it is often debates over differences of opinion, such as whether to legalize abortion, how to treat prisoners, or when to enact the death penalty, that shape our society and drive it forward. Such diversity of thought is frequently regarded as the hallmark of a healthy and civilized culture. As the Reverend Clifford Schutjer of the First Congregational Church in Mansfield, Ohio, declared in a 2001 sermon, "Surrounding oneself with only like-minded people, restricting what we listen to or read only to what we find agreeable is irresponsible. Refusing to entertain doubts once we make up our minds is a subtle but deadly form of arrogance." With this advice in mind, Introducing Issues with Opposing Viewpoints books aim to open readers' minds to the critically divergent views that comprise our world's most important debates.

Introducing Issues with Opposing Viewpoints simplifies for students the enormous and often overwhelming mass of material now available via print and electronic media. Collected in every volume is an array of opinions that captures the essence of a particular controversy or topic. Introducing Issues with Opposing Viewpoints books embody the spirit of nineteenth-century journalist Charles A. Dana's axiom: "Fight for your opinions, but do not believe that they contain the whole truth, or the only truth." Absorbing such contrasting opinions teaches students to analyze the strength of an argument and compare it to its opposition. From this process readers can inform and strengthen their own opinions, or be exposed to new information that will change their minds. Introducing Issues with Opposing Viewpoints is a mosaic of different voices. The authors are statesmen, pundits, academics, journalists, corporations, and ordinary people who have felt compelled to share their experiences and ideas in a public forum. Their words have been collected from newspapers, journals, books, speeches, interviews, and the internet, the fastest growing body of opinionated material in the world.

Introducing Issues with Opposing Viewpoints shares many of the well-known features of its critically acclaimed parent series, Opposing

Viewpoints. The articles allow readers to absorb and compare divergent perspectives. Active reading questions preface each viewpoint, requiring the student to approach the material thoughtfully and carefully. Photographs, charts, and graphs supplement each article. A thorough introduction provides readers with crucial background on an issue. An annotated bibliography points the reader toward articles, books, and websites that contain additional information on the topic. An appendix of organizations to contact contains a wide variety of charities, nonprofit organizations, political groups, and private enterprises that each hold a position on the issue at hand. Finally, a comprehensive index allows readers to locate content quickly and efficiently.

Introducing Issues with Opposing Viewpoints is also significantly different from Opposing Viewpoints. As the series title implies, its presentation will help introduce students to the concept of opposing viewpoints and learn to use this material to aid in critical writing and debate. The series' four-color, accessible format makes the books attractive and inviting to readers of all levels. In addition, each viewpoint has been carefully edited to maximize a reader's understanding of the content. Short but thorough viewpoints capture the essence of an argument. A substantial, thought-provoking essay question placed at the end of each viewpoint asks the student to further investigate the issues raised in the viewpoint, compare and contrast two authors' arguments, or consider how one might go about forming an opinion on the topic at hand. Each viewpoint contains sidebars that include at-a-glance information and handy statistics. A Facts About section located in the back of the book further supplies students with relevant facts and figures.

Following in the tradition of the Opposing Viewpoints series, Greenhaven Publishing continues to provide readers with invaluable exposure to the controversial issues that shape our world. As John Stuart Mill once wrote: "The only way in which a human being can make some approach to knowing the whole of a subject is by hearing what can be said about it by persons of every variety of opinion and studying all modes in which it can be looked at by every character of mind. No wise man ever acquired his wisdom in any mode but this." It is to this principle that Introducing Issues with Opposing Viewpoints books are dedicated.

Introduction

"The executive power shall be vested in a President of the United States of America. He shall hold his office during the term of four years, and, together with the Vice President, chosen for the same term, be elected, as follows: Each state shall appoint, in such manner as the Legislature thereof may direct, a number of electors, [which] shall meet in their respective states, and vote by ballot for two persons ... The person having the greatest number of votes shall be the President."

*—Constitution of the United States,
Article II, Section I*

The Founding Fathers of the United States faced a challenging position in the spring and summer of 1787. Finding their present form of government, the Articles of Confederation, unworkable, it was imperative that they fashion a new way to govern the country, including how to elect a president. Over a span of one hundred days, the delegates deliberated, discussed, hammered out a viable plan, and by September 17th, those assembled at the Constitutional Convention had adopted the Constitution of the United States. All these years later it is valuable to examine the controversy surrounding the Electoral College and the popular vote.

Many of the founders expressed concern during the debates over how the executive of the United States was to be elected. At the time of the Constitutional Convention, some of the delegates favored having the US Congress vote to elect the president, while others insisted that a popular vote of all the people should determine the nation's leader. Some argued that tyrants could be put into power by simple majority voting, while others battled over the issue of how smaller states should have equal representation and power as the largest states. James Madison, a representative from Virginia who recorded the proceedings in detailed accounts, stated that pure "democracies have ever been spectacles of turbulence and contention." Writing later in the Federalist Papers, he explained that if the founders had wanted a pure democracy rather than a republic they would have instituted the popular vote instead of an electoral college system to elect the president. And Alexander Hamilton spoke of the Electoral College that if "it be not perfect, it is at least excellent."

The Electoral College, as defined by *Merriam-Webster*, is "the body of electors chosen from each state to elect the president and vice president of the U.S." *Merriam-Webster* says, "The electors have the discretion to choose the candidate they vote for, but in practice the electors vote for the candidate that wins the most votes in their respective states."

Current debate over the Electoral College and the popular vote encompasses a wide proportion of people and ideas. Elected officials, people in juridical fields, potential candidates for office, union members, factory employees, shop owners, education professionals, everyday workers, students, and even those retired or unemployed demonstrate an interest in the presidential election process and have opinions about the fairness or appropriateness of the system. A Gallup Poll taken in 2011 indicated that 62 percent of Americans favored a change in the constitution to replace the Electoral College with a popular vote, and roughly 35 percent preferred to keep the system as it stands.

According to the US National Archives and Records Administration there have been more than seven hundred proposals brought forward in congress to abolish or amend the Electoral College system of voting. Groups and individuals differ in approach but basically settle into one of three factions: one group would keep the Electoral College, another would move to direct election, and the last segment is working to enact the National Popular Vote Interstate Compact. Each of the three options has both advantages and disadvantages, according to its proponents and challengers.

The Electoral College, as champions point out, is a major element of federalism and was designed and envisioned by the founders. For that reason alone, they argue, it deserves continuation. Seen as a compromise, it avoids simple majority vote, yet gives power to the public through the states. Proponents also refer to past elections to demonstrate the benefits of the Electoral College, and as a case in point, to the presidential election of 2000. In this closely contested race, the Electoral College provided political stability to the nation as there was doubt about which presidential candidate was the rightful winner. Simply put, it was less controversial to conduct a recount of Florida's votes—the state at the center of speculation—than having to recount the votes of the entire nation. This was possible because of the Electoral College system. Challengers decry the Electoral College as undemocratic, a holdover from the days of slavery, and at one time over 60 percent of US lawyers favored abolishing it, calling it "archaic and ambiguous."

Supporters of a direct election contend it is a simpler method of voting and infinitely more democratic. A candidate would need to rack up a clear majority of votes or obtain at least 40 percent to win an election. They also point out that every vote by all eligible voters would carry equal weight and importance, no matter where in the nation the ballot is registered. This method would also put all states on equal footing, with none at an advantage or disadvantage. Challengers maintain that direct elections would potentially cause political fragmentation, cause bitter post-election hassles, undermine public confidence, and cause small states to be almost totally ignored.

Proponents of the National Popular Vote Interstate Compact argue that voters in all states will have an equal say in the election of the president if this initiative passes. Under this system candidates will need to campaign across the nation, instead of devoting time and money to the typical twelve battleground states. The electoral votes of a state will be awarded to the winner of the state's popular vote, and consequently electors will no longer be needed. Critics contend that this system circumvents the constitution and ignores the amendment process set up by the founders. Additionally they point to Article 1, Section 10, Clause 3 of the US Constitution as a clear deterrent which states, "No State shall, without the Consent of Congress … enter into any Agreement or Compact with another State."

The current debate surrounding the system of electing the president in the United States is explored in *Introducing Issues with Opposing Viewpoints: The Electoral College and the Popular Vote*, shedding light on this divisive and ongoing contemporary issue.

Chapter 1

How Does the Electoral College Affect US Presidential Elections?

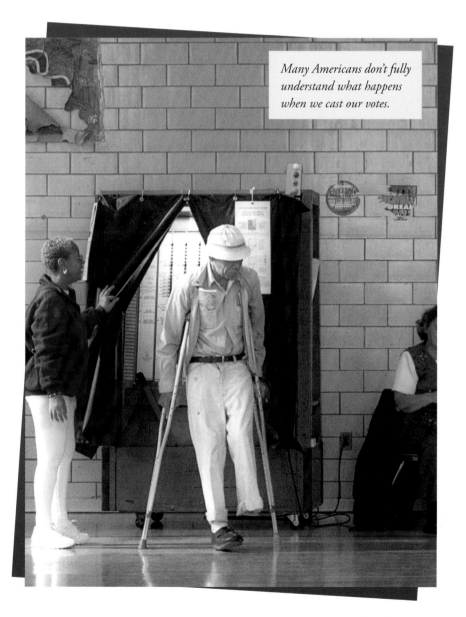

Many Americans don't fully understand what happens when we cast our votes.

The Electoral College Determines Presidential Elections

"The founding fathers established [the electoral college] in the Constitution as a compromise."

National Archives and Records Administration

In the following viewpoint, the National Archives and Records Administration (NARA) explains the foundation, makeup, and role of the Electoral College. The authors outline the creation of the Electoral College by the Founding Fathers and slight changes made to it via amendments. They describe the working of the Electoral College and its election of the US president, from election of electors to the ceremony in which the new president elect takes office. NARA is an organization that preserves all important documents and materials created by the US federal government and makes them available to the public.

AS YOU READ, CONSIDER THE FOLLOWING QUESTIONS:

1. Why did the Founding Fathers create the Electoral College?
2. Explain the makeup of the Electoral College.
3. How are Electoral College votes counted?

"What is the Electoral College?" U.S Electoral College, National Archives and Records Administration.

The Electoral College is a process, not a place. The founding fathers established it in the Constitution as a compromise between election of the President by a vote in Congress and election of the President by a popular vote of qualified citizens.

The Electoral College process consists of the selection of the electors, the meeting of the electors where they vote for President and Vice President, and the counting of the electoral votes by Congress.

The Electoral College consists of 538 electors. A majority of 270 electoral votes is required to elect the President. Your state's entitled allotment of electors equals the number of members in its Congressional delegation: one for each member in the House of Representatives plus two for your Senators. Read more about the allocation of electoral votes.

Under the 23rd Amendment of the Constitution, the District of Columbia is allocated 3 electors and treated like a state for purposes of the Electoral College. For this reason, in the following discussion, the word "state" also refers to the District of Columbia.

Each candidate running for President in your state has his or her own group of electors. The electors are generally chosen by the candidate's political party, but state laws vary on how the electors are selected and what their responsibilities are.

The presidential election is held every four years on the Tuesday after the first Monday in November. You help choose your state's electors when you vote for President because when you vote for your candidate you are actually voting for your candidate's electors.

Most states have a "winner-take-all" system that awards all electors to the winning presidential candidate. However, Maine and Nebraska each have a variation of "proportional representation."

Post-Election Action

After the presidential election, your governor prepares a "Certificate of Ascertainment" listing all of the candidates who ran for President in your state along with the names of their respective electors. The Certificate of Ascertainment also declares the winning presidential candidate in your state and shows which electors will represent your state at the meeting of the electors in December of the election year. Your state's Certificates of Ascertainments are sent to the Congress

The electoral votes are counted during a joint session of Congress.

and the National Archives as part of the official records of the presidential election.

The meeting of the electors takes place on the first Monday after the second Wednesday in December after the presidential election. The electors meet in their respective states, where they cast their votes for President and Vice President on separate ballots. Your state's electors' votes are recorded on a "Certificate of Vote," which is prepared at the meeting by the electors. Your state's Certificates of Votes are sent to the Congress and the National Archives as part of the official records of the presidential election.

Each state's electoral votes are counted in a joint session of Congress on the 6th of January in the year following the meeting of the electors. Members of the House and Senate meet in the House chamber to conduct the official tally of electoral votes. (On December 28, 2012, President Obama signed Pub.L. 112-228, as passed by both houses of Congress, moving the day of the vote count from January 6, 2013 (a Sunday) to January 4, 2013.)

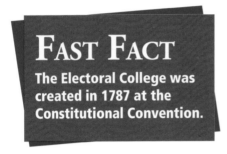

Fast Fact

The Electoral College was created in 1787 at the Constitutional Convention.

The Vice President, as President of the Senate, presides over the count and announces the results of the vote. The President of the Senate then declares which persons, if any, have been elected President and Vice President of the United States.

The President-Elect takes the oath of office and is sworn in as President of the United States on January 20th in the year following the Presidential election.

Roles and Responsibilities in the Electoral College Process

The Office of the Federal Register coordinates the functions of the Electoral College on behalf of the Archivist of the United States, the States, the Congress, and the American People. The Office of the Federal Register operates as an intermediary between the governors and secretaries of state of the States and the Congress. It also acts as a trusted agent of the Congress in the sense that it is responsible for reviewing the legal sufficiency of the certificates before the House and Senate accept them as evidence of official State action.

EVALUATING THE AUTHOR'S ARGUMENTS:

In this viewpoint the National Archives and Records Administration describes the Electoral College as a "compromise." Why do you think they consider it a compromise?

The Electoral College Once Protected Slavery

"I think if most Americans knew the origins of the Electoral College they would be disgusted."

Kamala Kelkar

In the following viewpoint Kamala Kelkar contends that the Electoral College was conceived in the era of slavery, by slave-holding founding fathers. In particular, Kelkar argues that James Madison, the "Father of the Constitution" concocted a plan in which slaves were counted as only three-fifths of a person. This was done in order to give Southern states the ability to influence presidential elections. Kelkar provides evidence that to this day federal courts are making it easier to restrict voting—a measure, the viewpoint contends, that is tied to the legacy of slavery. Kelkar is a journalist and a digital associate producer for *PBS NewsHour*.

AS YOU READ, CONSIDER THE FOLLOWING QUESTIONS:
1. What are the origins of the Electoral College as outlined in this viewpoint?
2. How was Thomas Jefferson able to beat John Adams in the election of 1800?
3. Cite an example of actions given by the viewpoint author that prevent voting by African Americans.

"Electoral College is 'Vestige' of Slavery, Say Some Constitutional Scholars," by Kamala Kelkar, @2016 News-Hour Productions LLC, November 6, 2016. Reprinted by permission.

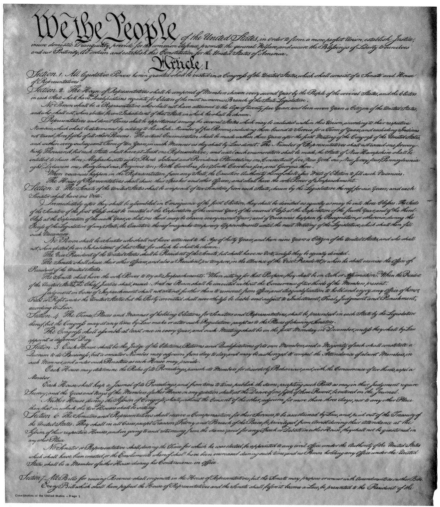

The Electoral College is embodied in Article 2, Section 1 of the US Constitution, as well as the Twelfth Amendment.

When the founders of the U.S. Constitution in 1787 considered whether America should let the people elect their president through a popular vote, James Madison said that "Negroes" in the South presented a "difficulty ... of a serious nature."

During that same speech on Thursday, July 19, Madison instead proposed a prototype for the same Electoral College system the country uses today. Each state has a number of electoral votes roughly proportioned to population and the candidate who wins the majority of votes wins the election.

Since then, the Electoral College system has cost four candidates the race after they received the popular vote—most recently in 2000, when Al Gore lost to George W. Bush. Such anomalies and other criticisms have pushed 10 Democratic states to enroll in a popular vote system. And while there are many grievances about the Electoral College, one that's rarely addressed is one dug up by an academic of the Constitution: that it was created to protect slavery, planting the roots of a system that's still oppressive today.

"It's embarrassing," said Paul Finkelman, visiting law professor at University of Saskatchewan in Canada. "I think if most Americans knew what the origins of the Electoral College is, they would be disgusted."

Madison, now known as the "Father of the Constitution," was a slave-owner in Virginia, which at the time was the most populous of the 13 states if the count included slaves, who comprised about 40 percent of its population.

During that key speech at the Constitutional Convention in Philadelphia, Madison said that with a popular vote, the Southern states, "could have no influence in the election on the score of Negroes."

Madison knew that the North would outnumber the South, despite there being more than half a million slaves in the South who were their economic vitality, but could not vote. His proposition for the Electoral College included the "three-fifths compromise," where black people could be counted as three-fifths of a person, instead of a whole. This clause garnered the state 12 out of 91 electoral votes, more than a quarter of what a president needed to win.

"None of this is about slaves voting," said Finkelman, who wrote a paper on the origins of the Electoral College for a symposium after Gore lost. "The debates are in part about political power and also the fundamental immorality of counting slaves for the purpose of giving political power to the master class."

He said the Electoral College's three-fifths clause enabled Thomas Jefferson, who owned more than a hundred slaves, to beat out in 1800 John Adams, who was opposed to slavery, since the South had a stronghold.

While slavery was abolished, and the Civil War led to citizenship and voting rights for black people, the Electoral College remained in-

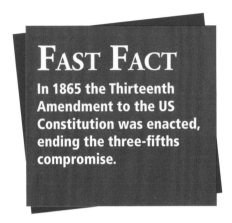

FAST FACT

In 1865 the Thirteenth Amendment to the US Constitution was enacted, ending the three-fifths compromise.

tact. Another law professor, who has also written that the Constitution is pro-slavery, argues that it gave states the autonomy to introduce discriminatory voting laws, despite the Voting Rights Act of 1965 that was built to prevent it.

In 2013, the Supreme Court freed nine states, mostly in the South, from the stipulation in the Voting Rights Act that said they could only change voter laws with the approval of the federal government.

"A more conservative Supreme Court has been unwinding what the [other] court did," said Juan Perea, a law Professor of Loyola University Chicago. "State by state, that lack of supervision and lack of uniformity operates to preserve a lot of inequality."

In July, a federal appeals court struck down a voter ID law in Texas, ruling that it discriminated against black and Latino voters by making it harder for them to access ballots. Two weeks later, another federal appeals court ruled that North Carolina, a key swing state, had imposed voting provisions that "target African Americans with almost surgical precision."

And for this presidential election, 15 states will have new voting restrictions, such as ones that require government-issued photo identification at the polls or reduce the number of hours the polls are open.

"The ability of states to make voting more difficult is directly tied to the legacy of slavery," Perea said. "And that ability to make voting more difficult is usually used to disenfranchise people of color."

The National Popular Vote Interstate Compact has gained traction, but for reasons more related to the anomaly of the Gore-Bush election. Assemblyman Jeffrey Dinowitz championed legislation in New York that brought the state into the compact and was asked by the NewsHour Weekend why the movement is important.

"We are the greatest democracy on the planet, and it seems to me that in the greatest democracy, the person who gets the most votes should win the election," said Dinowitz. "We're one country, North, South, East and West. One country. The votes of every single person in the country should be equal. And right now, the votes are not equal. Some states your vote is more important than in other states."

New York overwhelmingly agreed on his bill in 2014, joining nine other states and Washington, D.C. Together, they have 165 electoral votes. If they gain a total of 270 — the majority needed to elect a president — the nation will move to a popular vote.

Not all academics agree that slavery was the driving force behind the Electoral College, though most agree there's a connection. And both Perea and Finkelman say they know it is not the most prominent argument for the push toward a popular vote.

"But it is a vestige that has never been addressed," Perea said.

EVALUATING THE AUTHOR'S ARGUMENTS:

In this viewpoint Kamala Kelkar quotes a law professor, who asserts that most Americans would be disgusted to know the origins of the Electoral College. Do you think we should feel disgust over actions our ancestors took?

The Electoral College Protects Americans' Freedoms

"Rather than seeing the electoral college as old, antiquated or ineffective ... the process continues to protect Americans' freedoms."

Billy Hallowell

In the following viewpoint, Billy Hallowell outlines a case supporting the Electoral College and details the reasons behind the actions of the Founding Fathers in creating the system. Hallowell argues that the Electoral College system is not old or ineffective but rather an agency that protects and safeguards American freedoms. This is because the Electoral College is a blend of democracy and federalism. Hallowell reports on issues of culture and faith for *Deseret News National.*

AS YOU READ, CONSIDER THE FOLLOWING QUESTIONS:

1. According to the viewpoint what kind of government did the founders create?
2. How is the Electoral College a safeguard, as stated by the author?
3. Identify a drawback of the Electoral College given by critics, as stated by the author.

"Why Did the Founding Fathers Choose the Electoral College for Electing Presidents?" by Billy Hallowell, Deseret News, September 24, 2016. Reprinted by permission.

The Founding Fathers did not want to give too much voting power to the people.

What exactly is the electoral college—and why did the Founding Fathers embrace it instead of creating a direct presidential voting process?

These are just two questions that attorney and author Tara Ross—a staunch defender of the electoral college system—passionately answered in a recent appearance on "The Church Boys" podcast.

Ross recently released a kids book titled, "We Elect a President: The Story of Our Electoral College"—a follow-up to her nonfiction book for adults titled, "Enlightened Democracy: The Case for the Electoral College."

She argues in her writings and public addresses that the Founding Fathers were quite intentional in rejecting a direct electoral process.

"The most important thing to know about (the Founders) mind-set as they were crafting our entire constitution ... they were not try-

FAST FACT

The United States was not created as a pure democracy.

ing to create a pure democracy," Ross told "The Church Boys." "We live in a country that has democratic principles, but also republican principles (like deliberation and compromise)."

Some will surely wonder why a democratic system simply wasn't established, with Ross explaining, in her view, why the Founders rejected such a prospect.

"They knew that, in a pure democracy, 51 percent of the people can rule over 49 percent all the time without question, no matter how ridiculous their demands," she explained.

Ross said that the Founders studied history and knew that democracies could have pitfalls, so she said, "they wanted to do something better."

FactCheck.org agrees with this assessment as well.

"They solved their problem by creating a constitution with lots of checks and balances," she said. "The electoral college is just one of the safeguards ... it operates as a blend of democracy ... and federalism."

Rather than seeing the electoral college as old, antiquated or ineffective, Ross said the process continues to protect Americans' freedoms. The author also believes people tend to appreciate the process more as they learn how it all works.

So, let's briefly explain: According to the U.S. government, the electoral college serves as a "compromise between election of the president by a vote in Congress and choice of the president by a popular vote of qualified citizens."

The electoral college is made up of 538 electors, with a presidential contender needing to amass 270 electoral votes to win an election. The determination of electors for each state is based on how many members of Congress represent the state — a combination of the total of House members plus two Senators for each.

Electors are mostly chosen by political parties in each state, though the governing laws do differ when it comes to selection. Most states run on a "winner-takes-all" mentality.

Some who oppose the electoral college system argue that it gives small states too much power, as those smaller states might end up with three electoral college votes despite having only one representative in the House, *The Atlantic* reported.

Consider Montana, for example. While the state only has one representative, it still walks away with the three electoral college votes. There's also the issue of a candidate who gets just 51 percent of the popular vote, yet takes all the electoral college votes, as *The Atlantic* noted.

Let's not forget 2000 when Al Gore won the popular vote, yet George W. Bush secured an electoral college win in a narrow 271-266 victory.

But despite these concerns, Ross sees many benefits with the electoral college system, saying that it forces candidates to "build national coalitions" across state boundaries and that it makes it more difficult to steal elections.

"The reason the founders created the electoral college ... they knew that humans are imperfect," she said. "We are sinful ... they knew that power corrupts."

Ross concluded that the electoral college was created as a protection "against imperfect human nature."

EVALUATING THE AUTHOR'S ARGUMENTS:

In this viewpoint Billy Hallowell cites an author who claims that the Electoral College continues to protect Americans' freedoms. How would author Kamala Kelkar from the previous viewpoint react to Hallowell's assertions?

Viewpoint

4

Many Americans Believe the Electoral College Is Confusing and Unfair

"They envisioned that the electors would carefully discuss the qualifications of each candidate and engage in vigorous debate before casting their votes and sending them to Congress."

Geri Zabela Eddins

In the following excerpted viewpoint, Geri Zabela Eddins contends that, while perhaps recognized as imperfect, the Electoral College was the only presidential election system that the Founding Fathers could agree upon. Eddins points out that in some instances the Electoral College system can actually cause an individual to win the election but still lose the popular vote— something that has actually occurred in recent elections—and when this happens people become upset. Geri Zabela Eddins is a technical writer, editor, and assistant director at the National Children's Book and Literacy Alliance.

"Getting the Votes and Getting Elected: The Popular Vote vs. The Electoral College," by Geri Zabela Eddins, The National Children's Book and Literacy Alliance. Reprinted by permission.

1. According to Eddins, what are people actually voting for when they cast their ballot?
2. Explain the Founding Fathers' compromise according to the author.
3. Why did Congress ratify the Twelfth Amendment as noted in the viewpoint?

When we vote in November and mark our choices for president and vice president, we are actually voting for electors—people who represent our choices in the Electoral College. (The term Electoral College does not refer to an institution of higher learning, but to the group of representatives from each state who are pledged to vote for a particular candidate.) So, if our ballot reads "Jane Smith" and "John Doe," each vote for Smith is really a vote for an elector who has pledged his or her support for Smith.

Although the news media announce the probable winner the evening or morning following the November general election, the election is not official until the Electoral College votes and Congress has counted those votes. The chosen electors meet in December (on the first Monday after the second Wednesday) in their respective state capitals to cast their votes. The Constitution does not require electors to vote based on their state's popular vote; however, twenty-nine states do have their own laws that legally bind electors to cast their votes for their party's candidate. Sometimes electors do choose to write in the name of someone else or to abstain. For example, in the 2016 election between Republican candidate Donald J. Trump and Democratic candidate Hillary Clinton, a record-breaking seven electors chose not to cast votes for their pledged candidates. Such a large number of electors deviating from their pledged votes is highly unusual. To date no elector has ever been prosecuted for voting against his or her pledged candidate, and the constitutionality of the state laws governing the votes of electors has not yet been tested.

The votes cast by the electors in each state are sent to the president of the Senate to be counted before a joint session of Congress on January 6. The candidate who has received a majority of the 538

Strategy has become an essential factor in winning a presidential election. Candidates might devote more time to campaigning in states that offer more electoral votes.

possible electoral votes (which is at least 270) is declared president. The transfer of power to the new president occurs at noon on January 20 when he or she is sworn in by the Chief Justice of the Supreme Court.

In most election years, the workings of the Electoral College are a formality. Media outlets are able to "announce" the winner with near perfect accuracy based on the popular vote because the vast majority of electors do vote for their party's nominee. So today we almost always know the winner before the Electoral College meets.

Granting Electors

Article II of the Constitution grants each state the same number of electors to the Electoral College as it has Congressional representatives and senators. However, the Constitution does not stipulate rules that each state must follow in granting the electoral votes to presidential candidates. So, even though forty-eight states use a winner-take-all system (giving all its electoral votes to the candidate who receives the highest popular vote), the states of Maine and Nebraska do not. These two states grant their electoral votes based on the popular votes in each congressional district of their states. That means if a candidate receives the majority of votes in California, he or she will be awarded all fifty-five electoral votes. But if the same candidate does not win the majority in Nebraska, he or she can still gain one or two electoral votes if he or she wins one or more districts.

Winners and Losers

When a president wins the popular vote but still loses the presidency, people can become very upset. In fact, when this happened in 1876, the state of the union was so fragile that the U.S. was nearly plunged into a second civil war. This controversial election pitted Republican Rutherford B. Hayes against Democrat Samuel J. Tilden. Both candidates and parties were advocating for the same thing—government reform—so in order to differentiate their campaigns, both sides engaged in mudslinging and vicious attacks. Republicans accused Tilden of evading taxes and profiting by defending corrupt politicians. The Democrats countered by declaring Hayes had stolen the pay of soldiers who died in the Civil War. They also alleged that Hayes had even shot his own mother. The election was incredibly close, and newspapers initially reported that Tilden had won. At first it did seem that Tilden had won because he had secured 184 electoral votes and Hayes had won only 165. But, 185 electoral votes were needed to win the election, and the votes of four states became hotly contested. Congress appointed a commission of seven Democrats, seven Republicans, and one Independent to resolve the dispute. Unfortunately, the Independent candidate resigned and a Republican was appointed to replace him. This shifted the balance of the commission to eight Republicans and only seven Democrats. Not surprisingly, the commission voted along party lines and all electoral votes were awarded to Hayes. So, in the end, Tilden won the popular vote, but Hayes won the Electoral College and the election. Democrats condemned

FAST FACT

A presidential candidate must win at least 270 electoral votes to be declared president.

Hayes as "His Fraudulency" and "Rutherfraud B. Hayes," then took action. They armed themselves and threatened to secede. Tilden, however, kept his cool. He recognized the potential disaster and insisted that his supporters accept the decision. In the meantime, Democrats and Republicans also met secretly to negotiate a compromise—the Democrats would accept Hayes as president in return for certain concessions to the South, including the final removal of federal troops. Both sides agreed, and Hayes was inaugurated with the nation at peace.

Such drama is not unique to our country's earlier elections. The 2000 election was also a nail-biter, and the news media mistakenly declared the winner. At one point the Democrat Al Gore called his opponent Republican George W. Bush to concede. Later that evening, though, Gore learned that the votes in Florida were being deemed way too close to call, so he called Bush back to retract his concession. Bush was shocked, and so was the country as news reports surfaced with stories of voters who complained that their ballots were too confusing. Many voters were convinced they had voted incorrectly. The state of Florida was thrust into turmoil as it was forced to count and recount its votes into December after an automatic machine recount on November 14 revealed that Bush had won only 300 votes more than Gore in the almost six million total votes cast. Gore demanded a manual recount, but the recount produced an additional predicament. Many of the cardboard ballots had not been punched completely by voters, making it difficult for vote counters to determine the voters' intentions. Legal battles ensued all the way to the Supreme Court. The Supreme Court ultimately ruled that the manual recounts violated the Equal Protection Clause of the Fourteenth Amendment because the vote counters used different standards to determine how they counted each vote. By using different standards the recount was not treating all voters equally. They further ruled that it would be impossible to complete an accurate recount before the date required by the Constitution, so the Court stopped the count and awarded the votes to Bush. In this election, Gore won the popular vote by more than 500,000 votes, but his opponent Bush won the Electoral College and the election. Although many people throughout the country were outraged, this controversial election did not prompt calls for an armed revolution and Bush served two terms as president.

What Were They Thinking?! The Founding Fathers Compromise

If you think the Electoral College system is confusing and unfair, you are not alone. Many Americans share your opinion. In fact, over 700 proposals have been introduced in Congress over the last 200 years intending to either reorganize or eliminate the Electoral College. Even Thomas Jefferson wrote that he considered the Electoral College to be "the most dangerous blot in our Constitution." So, why do we elect our presidents this way? The simple answer is that the Electoral College was the best solution to selecting the president that the delegates at the Constitutional Convention could agree on. And this solution was a compromise.

Although Jefferson had written in the Declaration of Independence that "We hold these truths to be self-evident, that all men are created equal," the fact is that some of the delegates at the Constitutional Convention were skeptical about the ability of each American to cast an informed vote. Regarding the ability of the common man to vote, Massachusetts delegate Elbridge Gerry commented, "The people are uninformed, and would be misled by a few designing men." And Virginia delegate George Mason noted, "The extent of the country renders it impossible, that the people can have the requisite capacity to judge of the respective pretensions of the candidates." It is true that in the eighteenth century many people were uneducated and illiterate. Even by 1870—almost 100 years since America had declared its independence—20 percent of Americans continued to be illiterate. Other obstacles also prevented people from making informed decisions, such as geography; citizens were widely scattered, and many lived in remote locations. The lack of modern technology meant that mass communication did not exist. With no way to communicate information about potential candidates to all the voters—no radio, no TV, no Internet—the framers gave the voting power to electors, whose job it was to learn about the candidates, debate their qualifications when they met at the state capitals, and vote for us. Although giving the vote to Congress was also considered, the delegates ultimately decided this would grant the legislative body way too much power. So, creating the Electoral College became the compromise between those who favored a popular vote and those who favored allowing Congress to determine the president. Furthermore, instituting the Electoral College addressed one additional concern—the need to provide equity between states with large and small populations. By granting each state a number of electors equal to its representatives in Congress (which differs by state) and Senators (which is two, the same for each state), they hoped that more populous states would not exercise too much power in electing the president. Therefore, even a very small state is provided a minimum number of three electors.

Political Parties Compel Changes

When the delegates at the Constitutional Convention decided to create an Electoral College to choose the president, their vision for how this group would work was somewhat idealistic. In their minds, electors would be educated and distinguished citizens of each state who would be free to consider each presidential candidate. They envisioned that the electors would carefully discuss the qualifications of each candidate and engage in vigorous debate before casting their votes and sending them to Congress. And in our country's early elections the Electoral College did work this way because electors were chosen either by the state legislatures or by popular vote within each state. However, the development and rising power of political parties transformed this process from the Fathers' idealistic vision. Over time, electors were no longer chosen for their distinction as citizens, but for their loyalty to a particular party. Today, electors are chosen at state party conventions or are appointed directly by party leaders. Each major party elects or appoints the same number of electors as the state has electoral votes. So, when the electors chosen in the November election meet in their respective state capitols in December, there is no vigorous debate about the presidential candidates' qualifications—the electors simply vote for their party's candidate.

One additional departure from the Fathers' initial vision for presidential elections centers on how the votes are cast. Initially, each elector cast two votes but did not specify one as being for president and the other as being for vice president. The candidate with the most number of votes became president, and the candidate with the second highest number of votes became vice president. This system worked well for only our country's first two elections when Washington was elected unanimously. But in the midst of Washington's second term, political parties rose to power to influence the subsequent elections in unanticipated ways. The winners of the 1796 election—John Adams as president and Thomas Jefferson as his vice president—were members of opposing political parties. The following election hosted a rematch between the two, which provided the only election in American history in which a president ran against his vice president. In this election the Democratic Republican candidate Jefferson and running mate Aaron Burr each received the same number of votes. The tie sent the vote to the House of Representatives, which became deadlocked for days. Alexander Hamilton, who believed his fellow Federalist Adams was a dishonest man, exercised his own political muscle as a Federalist Party leader and influenced five other Federalists to withhold their votes so that Jefferson could win a majority. On the thirty-sixth ballot Jefferson was finally elected. To prevent similar predicaments from happening in the future, Congress ratified the Twelfth Amendment in 1804. This amendment requires separate votes for president and vice president and also stipulates that the president and vice president must come from different states.

[...]

EVALUATING THE AUTHOR'S ARGUMENTS:

In this viewpoint Geri Zabela Eddins reports that some voters become upset when a presidential candidate wins the Electoral College vote but loses the popular vote. How might those voters react to the statistics presented in the following viewpoint by Danielle Kurtzleben?

Viewpoint

5

The Electoral College Can Distort Election Results

"If the Electoral College disappeared tomorrow, campaign strategy would probably shift dramatically."

Danielle Kurtzleben

In the following viewpoint, Danielle Kurtzleben analyzes how the Electoral College can skew election results and presents statistics to back her claims. Kurtzleben convincingly presents mathematical analysis through charts and statistics demonstrating possible scenarios of presidential candidates winning the Electoral College by wide margins while winning the popular vote by as little as 27 percent. Kurtzleben is a political reporter who writes for National Public Radio's blog It's All Politics.

AS YOU READ, CONSIDER THE FOLLOWING QUESTIONS:

1. According to Kurtzleben, how can a presidential candidate win by winning only eleven states?
2. What is unusual in the race between Ronald Reagan and Walter Mondale as stated by Kurtzleben?
3. Why do some states get more attention from candidates than others according to the author?

©2016 National Public Radio, Inc. NPR news report "How To Win The Presidency With 23 Percent Of The Popular Vote" by Danielle Kurtzleben was originally published on npr.org on November 2, 2016, and is used with the permission of NPR. Any unauthorized duplication is strictly prohibited.

Donald Trump is not the first person to win the presidency without winning the popular vote, thanks to the electoral college.

I t's that time again: time for Americans to figure out how, exactly, their presidential election works. "Electoral College" searches spike every four years, just before Election Day, according to Google ... and the search volume is picking up right now.

Long story short: To win the presidency, you don't have to win the majority of the *popular* vote. You have to win the majority of *electoral* votes—that is, 270 of them. In most states, a candidate wins electoral votes by winning the most voters.

So. Win a state by just one vote, and you win all of its electoral votes (unless you live in Nebraska or Maine, which divvy up their votes a little differently).

This can lead to off-kilter election results—in 2000, for example, Democrat Al Gore won the popular vote by a few hundred thousand votes, but lost the presidency by five electoral votes. So we wondered: Just how few votes would a candidate need to win 270 electoral votes?

We decided to find out. A candidate only needs to win the 11 states with the most electoral votes to hit 270. Assuming only two candidates (a big assumption; see below) and that one candidate won all of those states by just one vote, and then didn't win a single vote in any of the other states (or D.C.), how many votes would that candidate have to win? It depends on how you do the math. Either way, it's far less than half.

Initially when we did this story, we found that if you start with the biggest-electoral-vote states, the answer is 27 percent. However, we have an update: as Andrej Schoeke very nicely pointed out to us on Twitter, there's another way to do it (via CGP Grey) that requires even less of the popular vote: start with the smallest-electoral-vote states. Our math went through a few iterations on this but by our final math, in 2012 that could have meant winning the presidency with only around 23 percent of the popular vote.

The idea here is that a voter in a low-population state like Wyoming counts for a larger share of electoral votes than popular votes.

And if one were to start with the largest states, it would be 27 percent.

We're making a lot of assumptions here—we're using vote totals from 2012, for one thing. Moreover, we're assuming there are only two candidates in the race.

And let's be clear about the obvious here: This kind of an extreme election isn't going to happen. And if it did—if there were somehow a bunch of 1- or 2-vote wins, you can bet the recounts would stretch into 2017.

And we're also sure that with any number of tweaks to the math (like plugging in a third or fourth candidate), you could come up with results that are slightly-to-moderately different. But that's not really the point here. The point is that the Electoral College can skew election results to a fantastic degree.

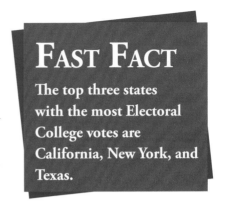

FAST FACT

The top three states with the most Electoral College votes are California, New York, and Texas.

How a 7-point Win Becomes a "Landslide"

This kind of popular-electoral vote discrepancy is why some articles about the 2008 election had to be careful to call Obama's win an *electoral* landslide—he won 68 percent of the electoral vote but only about 53 percent of the popular vote.

Skewed wins like this happen regularly in U.S. elections—a modest popular vote margin can yield a ridiculously large Electoral College margin. For example, in 1984, Ronald Reagan beat Walter Mondale in the popular vote by 18 points—a sizable gap, but nothing like the Electoral College walloping: Reagan won 525 electoral votes, beating Mondale by 95 percentage points.

The chart on the next page shows what those gaps look like in every election going back to 1960's race, in which John F. Kennedy only squeaked past Richard Nixon in the popular vote by around 100,000 votes.

Ironically, the 2000 election—whose outcome struck many people as unfair because Gore won the popular vote but not the electoral vote—also has the electoral-vote margin that most closely reflects the popular-vote margin. In that sense, one could call it one of the "fairest" elections in modern politics.

Well, maybe. But then, come Nov. 9, there will be no difference for the losing candidate between getting 250 electoral votes or 150—a loss is a loss.

The Difference an Electoral College Makes

The Electoral College and current demographics mean that both par-

The Electoral College Turns Modest Wins Into Landslides

Presidential election victors often win by a larger margin in the Electoral College than in the popular vote. Notably, in 1984, Ronald Reagan beat Walter Mondale by about 18 percentage points in the popular vote (winning 59 percent of the vote to Mondale's 41), but by 95.2 percentage points in the Electoral College (with 97.6 percent of the electoral vote [525] to Mondale's 2.4 percent [13]). Below are the winning candidate's margin of victory in the popular vote and Electoral College for each election year since 1960:

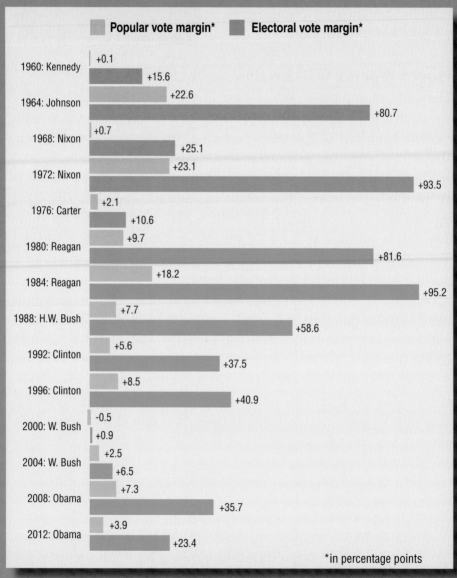

Popular vote margin*   **Electoral vote margin***

- 1960: Kennedy — +0.1 / +15.6
- 1964: Johnson — +22.6 / +80.7
- 1968: Nixon — +0.7 / +25.1
- 1972: Nixon — +23.1 / +93.5
- 1976: Carter — +2.1 / +10.6
- 1980: Reagan — +9.7 / +81.6
- 1984: Reagan — +18.2 / +95.2
- 1988: H.W. Bush — +7.7 / +58.6
- 1992: Clinton — +5.6 / +37.5
- 1996: Clinton — +8.5 / +40.9
- 2000: W. Bush — -0.5 / +0.9
- 2004: W. Bush — +2.5 / +6.5
- 2008: Obama — +7.3 / +35.7
- 2012: Obama — +3.9 / +23.4

*in percentage points

Source: Dave Leip's Election Atlas
Credit: Danielle Kurtzleben/NPR

ties often take particular electoral votes for granted: Democrats regularly win California and New York, while Republicans win Texas and Georgia (however, things have been closer than usual in those states this year).

(Likewise, there are plenty of easy wins for each party at the low end of the spectrum. Wyoming is regularly Republican. Hawaii regularly votes Democratic.)

And that means that candidates regularly spend a disproportionate amount of time in high-electoral-vote battleground states like Florida and Ohio as they plot their "paths to 270." This means voters in Los Angeles or San Antonio (or Cheyenne or Honolulu) don't get that much attention.

If the Electoral College disappeared tomorrow, campaign strategy would probably shift dramatically; Democrats might campaign more in Austin, Texas. Republicans might do more outreach in conservative parts of California. Either way, the people of Ohio, Florida and Pennsylvania might get some respite from the onslaught of rallies and ads every four years, as candidates try harder to win bigger parts of the country.

EVALUATING THE AUTHOR'S ARGUMENTS:

In this viewpoint Danielle Kurtzleben presents various scenarios where a presidential candidate can win the Electoral College vote with a small percentage of the popular vote. Does this impact your opinion of the fairness of the Electoral College?

Chapter 2

Does the Popular Vote Matter in US Presidential Elections?

★ BE RESPONSIBLE ★

YOUR VOTE MATTERS

★ ELECTION 2016 ★

Some voters believe their votes are inconsequential.

The Electoral College Makes My Vote Irrelevant

"There's no shorter way to tearing a country in half than making sure half of its electorate feels entirely unrepresented."

Scott Santens

In the following viewpoint, written just before the 2016 presidential election, Scott Santens argues that the Electoral College undermines our participation in elections. If the less popular presidential candidate can come out the winner, he asserts, then why should we bother to vote at all? The author suggests supporting the National Popular Vote bill, under which states would pledge to apportion their electors by popular vote, thus ensuring our votes can make a difference. Santens is a journalist whose work has been featured in the *Atlantic*, *Forbes*, Politico, the Huffington Post, and the *Boston Globe*.

AS YOU READ, CONSIDER THE FOLLOWING QUESTIONS:

1. How would implementation of the National Popular Vote bill improve our election system, according to the author?
2. What is ranked choice, and why does the author think it might be an improvement?
3. What reasons does the author give for suggesting election day be a national holiday?

"How to Make Our Votes for President of the United States Actually Count," by Scott Santens, Medium, November 2, 2016. https://medium.com/@2noame/how-to-make-our-votes-for-president-of-the-united-states-actually-count-d246021d1808. Licensed under CC-BY SA 4.0.

Each state's allotment of electors is determined by the number of members in the state's congressional delegation. That equals one for each member in the House and one for each senator.

After what feels like the longest election in the history of the United States, Election Day 2016 is finally coming up on November 8th, and once again, because of the Electoral College system and how it works, for the majority of citizens, myself included, our votes won't actually matter.

We don't actually vote for President. We vote to suggest to a group of 538 electors who we think they should vote for. Not only that, but each state's electors (with the exception of Nebraska and Maine) are winner take all, which has some surprisingly undemocratic consequences.

Yep, we've got a big problem. We like to pretend we have a democracy, but we don't. Whoever gets the most votes, does not necessarily win. In fact, because of the Electoral College, it's actually theoretically possible for someone to lose after getting 78% of the popular vote to someone who only got 21.91% of the popular vote.

As if it's not bad enough that someone so wanted by the overwhelming majority of the country could ever be beaten by someone the country absolutely doesn't want, thanks to our peculiar use of electors, I would argue its effect on our participatory democracy is even worse, because it begs the question, "What's the point?"

Take my state for example. I live in Louisiana. According to the latest polls on FiveThirtyEight, there is a 99.5% chance that Trump will win this state, and therefore all 8 of this state's electoral votes. The thing is, if he won with one vote over 50% of the vote, he'd still get all 8 electoral votes, and therefore the votes of anyone above that mark don't matter. If you vote for Trump or you vote for Hillary, it really doesn't matter because this state is not even close to being a swing state. It's a decided-in-advance state.

The situation is different in Florida where there are 29 electoral votes up for grabs, and a 51% chance currently that Hillary will win them versus a 49% chance that Trump will. That's basically a flip of a coin, and so in Florida every vote counts because even one vote could sway the election, and all its 29 electors along with it.

It doesn't have to be this way though. And it arguably shouldn't because someone barely winning all of the votes is another way of saying the people are in a state of maximum disagreement. There's no shorter way to tearing a country in half than making sure half of its electorate feels entirely unrepresented.

Thankfully, the Constitution allows each state to allocate its electors however they see fit, so if all states apportioned their electors according to their respective popular votes, a really close election in Florida could result in 15 electors voting for the winner and 14 electors for the loser. Someone barely winning is thereby reflected in the results and more people feel represented.

Meanwhile, back here in Louisiana, it could mean 5 votes going to Trump and 3 votes going to Hillary. Because electors would be allocated based on percentage, it would incentivize everyone to vote just like being a swing state incentivizes everyone in Florida to vote. It's the difference between your vote being heard, and your vote being silenced. Winner-take-all is a bad idea.

The trick though, and why this seemingly simple fix to a flawed system hasn't been enacted yet, is because to do it one by one could flip elections for decades to come. Imagine if California decided to apportion its electors by popular vote and 49% voted Republican.

That would mean an extra 27 electoral votes for Republicans and 27 fewer electoral votes for Democrats going forward. And the same is true for a state like Texas, but the other way around.

However, some bright people have figured out a way around this quandary, and it's called the National Popular Vote bill. Basically, it's like a Kickstarter for democracy, where state after state pledges to apportion their electors by popular vote, but only after enough states all together pledge to do so, such that the sum total of their electors reaches the 270 electoral votes required for a candidate to win the presidency. Clever, isn't it?

If we care about democracy, and if we want everyone's vote to count each time we go to the polls to choose our next president, we'll do this. We'll contact our representatives and we'll demand they support it. And if we don't, we'll just keep on making every Election Day mostly pointless for all states but swing states.

Election 2020

So is there a way to make our votes count this year if we happen to live in a solid "red" or "blue" state like Louisiana? Yes, there is. The results of the national popular vote do actually matter for something, but not for this presidential election. They matter for the next presidential election.

Here's the thing. If a candidate gets 5% of the popular vote nationally, that party's candidate will qualify for federal matching funds the next time around. Basically, we may not have a democracy when it comes to the presidency, but we do have a democracy when it comes to deciding which political parties get money, and therefore which parties get on all the ballots, and therefore most importantly, which third parties are seen as threats.

> *Their function has not been to win or govern, but to agitate, educate, generate new ideas, and supply the dynamic element in our political life. When a third party's demands become popular enough, they are appropriated by one or both of the major parties and the third party disappears. Third parties are like bees: once they have stung, they die.*
>
> *—Richard Hofstadter*

So if you want your vote to matter if you happen to not live in an all-votes matter swing state, vote for a third party. If that party gets 5% of the popular vote nationwide, the policies of its platform are more likely to be added to the platforms of the two main parties out of fear of losing votes to them next time around. You have nothing to fear in a solid red or blue state. You can vote strategically.

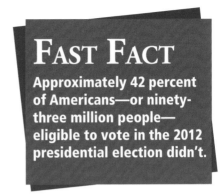

FAST FACT

Approximately 42 percent of Americans—or ninety-three million people— eligible to vote in the 2012 presidential election didn't.

For me personally, as a US citizen residing in Louisiana, my vote will be going to the Green Party in hopes I can help it get federal matching funding in 2020, because the two most important issues to me are taking action on climate change and adopting universal basic income. Both are part of the Green Party platform. For anyone who might get upset with that, again, there is a near-zero chance of Hillary winning my state and a virtual lock for Trump. The only way for my vote for President to actually matter is by popular vote.

By the way, there are a lot of other great ideas out there to strengthen our democracy than just making sure we reform our Electoral College system so that the electoral votes of each state are not winner take all.

Fair Representation

The way we draw our districts are simply insane. Gerrymandering is destructive to democracy. Our districts should be redrawn in a way that makes sense, and our representatives should represent who we actually are. We need fair representation.

Ranked Choice

Ranked choice voting or (instant runoff) is also a key part of the democratic reform we need. Third parties should never be considered spoilers. We should always be able to vote for who we most want to represent us, in a way that doesn't make it more likely for someone to win who we'd never want to represent us.

There are even more and better ideas than this, but ranked choice would be a definite improvement. Another big improvement would be allowing everyone to vote in our primaries.

Open Primaries

43% of the country considers itself as independent and yet in all states with closed primaries, they aren't allowed to vote in the primaries unless they pick a party they don't feel actually represents them. This is hugely problematic because their taxes are paying for the elections they aren't allowed to vote in. But even worse than that, the result is that those with extreme views win primaries, because they are trying to win the support of their respective bases instead of the independent voters that aren't allowed to vote for them. Then come the general election, independents are forced to choose among two candidates they never would have voted for, had they been allowed to vote previously. Closed primaries are a recipe for bad government.

Election Holiday

Finally, perhaps the most common sense improvement of all, is to simply make it easier for people to vote. Make it a national holiday or move it to the weekend. Or both, by moving it to a Friday or a Monday and making it a three-day weekend.

If we can't take the day off, at least allow everyone to vote by mail. Let's stop putting up barriers to voting by pretending voter ID laws are a good idea. They're not. They didn't even exist before 2006 and are a blatant attempt to engineer election outcomes through selective disenfranchisement.

Our goal should be to grow and strengthen our democracy over time. The changes we can make that will empower more people to vote and make sure their voices are actually counted and heard are the changes we need. Anything we do to prevent that or even go in the other direction are dangerous and should be reconsidered.

Don't be fooled into protecting the status quo. It is in the interest of our two major parties to claim voting for anyone else but them is a wasted vote. That they don't immediately do something like implement ranked-choice voting after each election to make sure that no one's vote serves as a "spoiler" the next time around simply goes to show they want it this way. They want you to feel forced to vote R or D, red or blue. They even want you to only vote against who you don't like instead of who you actually want, because if all you're voting for is against something, they never have to support what you're for.

Democracy is not a country of red and blue. Democracy is essentially purple. It's also green, and orange, and yellow, and all the rest. This is the country we actually live in, and if we want to "make it great again" improving our elections to be more democratic should be front and center. And considering the ideals our country was founded upon, no one, no matter how conservative or liberal, should be against the idea that voting is perhaps the most important right of citizenship, and even the price of freedom itself.

This is America. Let's make all our votes actually count.

> **EVALUATING THE AUTHOR'S ARGUMENTS:**
>
> In this viewpoint, author Scott Santens offers several ways the US election process could be improved. Do you think any of these have a possibility of being implemented? Why or why not?

Viewpoint

2

The Popular Vote Should Elect the President

Frank J. Lysy

"Doing away with the electoral college and electing the president by popular vote is overwhelmingly favored by the population."

In the following excerpted viewpoint, Frank J. Lysy argues that the current Electoral College system of voting is without a doubt not a democratic system. The author further argues that no other country where the president is the head of the executive branch of government is elected through a system that is not a popular vote of the entire nation. The author asserts that reform would benefit both major parties, but neither seems to recognize that fact. Frank J. Lysy blogs at AnEconomicSense.org and is former chief economist and director of the economics and policy group at the World Bank Group.

AS YOU READ, CONSIDER THE FOLLOWING QUESTIONS:

1. As stated by this author, identify the three main problems with the current electoral vote system.
2. How would a candidate's campaign change if the popular vote decided the winner?
3. What would be the benefits of a national popular vote according to the author?

"Bringing Democracy to America: The Popular Vote Should Determine Who Wins the Presidency," An Economic Sense, September 9, 2016. Reprinted by permission.

Many Americans agree that the electoral college should give way to the popular vote.

Introduction

The US is once again in the middle of a presidential election, with possible consequences this time that are more worrying than ever. [...] This is a consequence of the unique US system where presidents are selected not by who receives the most votes in the nation, but rather by who wins a plurality of votes in individual states whose electoral college votes sum to 270 or more (i.e. more than half of the total 538 electoral votes allocated across the nation). It does not matter if the candidate wins the state by a little or a lot; they receive the same number of electoral votes from the state regardless.

[...]

This is not a democratic system, and no other democratic country in the world with a president with substantial real powers selects their president this way. There are systems in some countries with a parliamentary form of government (where the party with a majority of seats in the parliament selects the prime minister) that might be seen as somewhat similar to an electoral college. But in such situations, the president is largely or totally a figurehead. In no other democratic country where the president is the head of the executive branch, other than the US, does one select that president other than through a popular vote of the entire nation.

[...]

The Problems With the Current Electoral College System

It is Not Democracy

To start, the current system is not democratic. Electoral votes are allocated by state to be equal to the number of congressmen from that state plus two (equal to the number of senators from each state). There are 538 electoral votes, the sum of 435 Congressmen, 100 Senators, and 3 electoral votes granted to Washington, DC, by the 23rd amendment to the Constitution (ratified in 1961).

The result is that voters in a state like Wyoming, a small state with fewer voters even than Washington, DC, have a disproportionate share of influence in the electoral college and hence in the selection of the president. In 2012, the voting-eligible population (VEP, equal to the voting age population of the state, less non-citizens and felons ineligible to vote) of Wyoming was 425,142. With 3 electoral votes, Wyoming had 141,714 voters per electoral vote.

In contrast, the voting-eligible population of California in 2012 was 23,681,837 for 55 electoral votes. Thus there were 430,579 voters in California for each of its electoral votes. That is, there were almost exactly 3 times as many voters in California per electoral vote as there were in Wyoming. Each vote in California counted only one-third as much. This is not democracy. In a democracy, each vote counts the same.

A Candidate Can Be Elected President Even Though He or She Received Fewer Votes

Directly following from the fact the current system is not democratic, is the possible consequence that whomever receives the most votes might not win the presidency. It is worth flagging this separately only because many believe that while this is theoretically possible, in practice it has been and would be so rare that we should not worry about it.

The results of the 2 00 election between George Bush and Al Gore did serve to wake people up that this result is indeed possible in modern times. Al Gore won the nation-wide popular vote over Bush by a not so small 0.5% points (544,000 votes), but lost due to a loss in Florida.

Furthermore, the loss in Florida was by just 537 votes, or 0.01% of the votes cast in that state.

[…]

And it is in fact not so rare that there might be an election where the winner of the electoral vote lost the popular vote. Aside from the 2000 election, there were three other such cases in American history (although all were in the 1800s). Thus in the 48 presidential elections since 1824 (the first election where, as discussed above, the popular vote at the state level was meaningful), there have been four cases where the person elected president received fewer votes than his opponent. That is, in one of 12 cases (4 in 48) the loser of the popular vote still became president. One in 12 cases means, on average, that one might expect there to be such a case every 48 years or so,

Do Away with Electoral College	In Favor	Opposed	No Opinion
All	63%	29%	8%
Republicans	61%	30%	9%
Independents	63%	29%	8%
Democrats	66%	30%	4%

Source: Gallup Poll, January 2013

given the four-year presidential terms. That is, each voter should expect this to happen about once in their voting lifetimes. That is not uncommon.

[…]

People Want the President to be Selected by Popular Vote

Finally, doing away with the electoral college and selecting the president by popular vote is overwhelmingly favored by the population. As the above table illustrates, a Gallup Poll from January 2013 found that 63% are in favor of such a reform.

[…]

The National Popular Vote Interstate Compact

While the problems with the electoral college system have long been recognized, most (including myself) thought until recently that a constitutional amendment would be required to change it. But in fact that is not so. Following the 2000 election debacle, Professor Roger

Bennett of Northwestern University Law School pointed out that the US Constitution (in its Article II, Section 1, Paragraph 2, quoted above) gives state legislatures the power to decide how electors will be chosen in their state. States could use this power to choose a slate of electors pledged not to the presidential candidate who received the most votes within their own state, but rather pledged to the presidential candidate who received the most votes in the nation.

[…]

The Benefits of a Selecting the President by National Popular Vote

The benefits of selecting the president by a national popular vote are clear, and include:

1. It is democratic.
2. Votes would count the same across the nation. Currently, a vote in California counts only one-third as much as a vote in Wyoming in terms of electoral votes.
3. It would end the possibility that a candidate receiving more votes than another would nonetheless lose the election, as happened in Bush vs. Gore in 2000 and three other times in US history.

[…]

But perhaps the biggest concrete impact would be the impact of such a reform on how candidates run for office. Instead of focusing almost all of their attention on a limited number of swing states, they would now have a reason to campaign across the entire nation. Their aim would be to pick up votes wherever they can. Thus a Republican would want to campaign in states like California, New York, and Massachusetts. While he might not expect to win a majority in such a state, there are a large number of potential Republican voters in such states whom he would want to encourage to go out and vote. Similarly, a Democrat would have an incentive to campaign in states like Texas and Alabama. Their aim would be to campaign wherever they might gain a significant number of votes, including in states where they might well still expect not to receive a majority overall.

FAST FACT

In 2016, less than half of Americans reported that they wanted to replace the Electoral College with a popular vote, according to a Gallup poll.

This would change the dynamics of US presidential campaigns, and in a good way. Three-quarters of the nation would not be neglected.

[...]

Conclusion

The electoral college system might well have made sense in 1788, when the US Constitution was ratified. But that does not mean it makes sense now. While a formal constitutional amendment might well be a preferable solution, the current politics in Washington means that any amendment process would not go far.

But the US Constitution does specifically provide the state legislatures the flexibility to decide how their electors are to be chosen. States can use that flexibility to direct that the slate of electors for that state will be the slate committed to the candidate who receives the most votes in the nation, rather than in the individual state. And the states can agree that they will begin to abide by this process when, and only when, states with a minimum of 270 electoral college votes have agreed.

This is thus eminently doable. However, while states with 165 electoral votes have already approved this initiative, there is a need for states with a further 105 electoral votes also to agree. This will not happen until Republican controlled states recognize that this reform is as much in their interest as it is for others.

EVALUATING THE AUTHOR'S ARGUMENTS:

In this viewpoint the author favors a change in the US presidential election voting system. Compare this author's viewpoint with the one presented by Scott Santens.

The United States Is Not a Democracy

Matt Peppe

"In a true democracy, anyone who was subject to the rule of a government would enjoy the rights of citizenship and democratic participation."

In the following viewpoint, Matt Peppe examines the roots of the Electoral College and questions whether the United States is a democracy. Peppe notes that America's Founding Fathers went to great lengths to ensure that their new nation was not a true democracy, because they wanted the decision making to be in the hands of an educated, elite group rather than all of the people. Peppe argues that since so many groups, such as African Americans and women, have been denied the right to vote in America's past (and some in the present, as well), the United States should not be known around the world as a democracy. Matt Peppe writes about politics for the online magazine CounterPunch.

AS YOU READ, CONSIDER THE FOLLOWING QUESTIONS:

1. According to the author, where did the idea of democracy originate and why?
2. How did the US Constitution as written by the Founding Fathers keep power within an elite class according to Peppe?
3. Identify those groups unable to vote as stated in this viewpoint.

"Is the United States Even a Democracy?" by Matt Peppe, first appeared on www.CounterPunch.org, August 12, 2014. Reprinted by permission.

Everyone in the world knows that the government of the United States is a democracy, and that the United States stands for promoting democracy around the world. How do we know this is true? Because the government says so, all the time.

"Democracy and respect for human rights have long been central components of U.S. foreign policy," claims the State Department. "Supporting democracy not only promotes such fundamental American values as religious freedom and worker rights, but also helps create a more secure, stable and prosperous global arena in which the United States can advance its national interests."

Idealists would say this is a very benevolent sounding notion. Realists might say it is vacuous and inane. But the media, textbooks, even human rights organizations choose to propagate the idealistic version and claim as an article of faith that the United States does not just practice democracy, but embodies the very idea itself.

Democracy is used as a justification for everything the government does—domestically and abroad. Since the U.S. is the embodiment of democracy and democracy is good, then everything the U.S. does is good, by definition.

But it's not very often that anyone bothers to actually analyze this. Other than being an abstract concept, what actually is democracy and how does the U.S. fit this definition? As most people know, democracy comes from the ancient Greeks. It means power to the people. In Athenian democracy, people participated in governmental decision making by directly participating, with a majority vote used to determine how to act. Even in this system, only free males were granted the right of citizenship and participation in government so it was not a true democracy.

A true democracy would grant voting rights to all citizens – and no one would be denied citizenship because they were considered property. Neither should race, gender, religion, ethnicity or any other factor prevent someone from attaining citizenship and exercising their right to participate in government. In a true democracy, anyone who was subject to the rule of a government—and of adult age— would enjoy the rights of citizenship and democratic participation.

When the U.S. Constitution was drafted in 1787, the Founding Fathers took pains to ensure the new government would not be a

Drafter of the US Constitution James Madison was no fan of democracies.

democracy. They would create a government that bore some resemblance to democracy, but left the true decision making power in the hands of a small, elite group of men, who were better equipped to rule than the majority of the population.

Fast Fact

Citizens of the US territories cannot vote in presidential elections unless they move to the United States.

James Madison, who drafted the document that the final draft of the Constitution was modeled on, made no secret of his disdain for democracy.

"If a faction consists of less than a majority, relief is supplied by the republican principle, which enables the majority to defeat its sinister views by regular vote. It may clog the administration, it may convulse the society; but it will be unable to execute and mask its violence under the forms of the Constitution," Madison wrote in The Federalist No. 10. "When a majority is included in a faction, the form of popular government, on the other hand, enables it to sacrifice to its ruling passion or interest both the public good and the rights of other citizens. To secure the public good and private rights against the danger of such a faction, and at the same time to preserve the spirit and the form of popular government, is then the great object to which our inquiries are directed."

So in other words, the question for the Founding Fathers was how to protect the elites from the tyranny of the majority while maintaining a facade of popular rule? Madison's solution was a "republic, by which I mean a government in which the scheme of representation takes place." A republic, further, would be better at "controlling the effects of faction."

Madison meant that there needed to be a mechanism to control an opinion that was out of the control of elite interest, regardless of whether this opinion belonged to a majority. "By a faction, I understand a number of citizens, whether amounting to a majority or a minority of the whole, who are united and actuated by some common impulse of passion, or of interest, adversed to the rights of other citizens, or to the permanent and aggregate interests of the community."

The Constitution that emerged was able to achieve the delicate balance of some popular representation while keeping the true decision making power within the capable and deserving elite cabal. The House of Representatives would be the minor half of the lawmaking body of Congress. Its members would be elected by popular vote. The Senate would be the truly powerful body, with sole power over foreign policy for example, and that would not be representative. Each state would get 2 Senators, whether that state has 10 residents or 10 million. Further, the Senators would not be elected by the public. They would be chosen by the State Legislatures.

The President, the single most powerful member of the government, would be chosen by the vote of delegations of the State Legislatures. There would be a popular vote, sure, but it is non-binding. So if, for instance, 213 years later a son of a former President lost the popular election he could still become President even though another person had a higher number of votes.

So, fundamentally the U.S. government was designed to *not* be a democracy. It was designed to be a vehicle for white property owners to protect their interests—namely, their property and their right to perpetuate their ownership of it while those with less remained with less.

They would probably be pleased to know that several hundred years later their governmental experiment is fulfilling its purpose to perfection.

In a recent study, researchers at Princeton University and Northwestern University concluded that U.S. policymaking favors the wealthy and special interests groups more than average citizens. In fact, the wishes of average citizens are hardly represented by their elected representatives, if at all.

"Not only do ordinary citizens not have *uniquely* substantial power over policy decisions; they have little or no independent influence on policy at all," write Martin Gilens and Benjamin Page.

"We believe that if policymaking is dominated by powerful business organizations and a small number of affluent Americans, then America's claims to being a democratic society are seriously threatened," they conclude.

Of course, a look at the historical record showed this was actual the intent of the Founding Fathers all along.

Maybe because of the transparent lack of actual democratic mechanisms and institutions, the United States eventually began to narrow the definition of democracy essentially to one thing: the right to vote.

William Blum writes that this sense of the word was developed as propaganda to criticize Communist governments who considered things such as food, health care and education fundamental human rights. But they didn't have regular elections. So our system, with its glorious box checking, became "democracy" while theirs was "totalitarianism," Blum explains.

"Thus, a nation with hordes of hungry, homeless, untended sick, barely literate, unemployed, and/or tortured people, whose loved ones are being disappeared and/or murdered with state connivance, can be said to be living in a 'democracy' ... provided that every two years or four years they have the right to go to a designated place and put an X next to the name of one or another individual who promises to relieve their miserable condition, but who will, typically, do virtually nothing of the kind."

It has taken an Orwellian perversion of the English language to claim that countries like Venezuela and Cuba, who practice versions of grassroots, direct democratic groups like people's councils and trade unions, are not part of democracy if they don't have multi-party elections.

As this is really the sole basis of U.S. claims to democracy you would think it would be a valid claim. But you would be wrong. The truth is that in the history of the nation, there has not been even *one single day* where all voting-age United States citizens were allowed to vote in federal elections!

At the time of the Constitution, only land-owning white males were allowed to vote. This obviously left out landless whites, all women, and all African Americans. This was true until the Civil War.

"In 1860, just five states limited suffrage to taxpayers and only two still imposed property qualifications," writes Steven Mintz.

So at this point, no African Americans or women had the right to vote. Shortly after, with the ratification of the Fifteenth Amendment, African Americans were granted the nominal right to vote. However, poll taxes, literacy tests and other obstacles were used especially in the South to ensure that freed slaves were not able to exercise that right—at least in more than small numbers. It was not until the Civil Rights Act in 1964 that this type of disenfranchisement was federally prohibited.

buts and ifs and ors. Surely the cross on a piece of paper does not express them ... [C]alling a vote the expression of our mind is an empty fiction.

There have been 57 presidential elections. By my count, 12 of them elected candidates that were almost certainly not the true choices of the electorate, the last three occurring in 1912, 1992 and 2000.

Woodrow Wilson was elected in 1912 (with 41.8 percent of the popular vote) against incumbent Republican President William Howard Taft (23.2 percent) because of the Bull Moose candidacy of the former Republican President Teddy Roosevelt (27.4 percent): Either of them would most likely have won head-to-head against Wilson.

A similar scenario occurred in 1992 with Bill Clinton (43.0 percent) winning against George H. W. Bush (37.4 percent) because of the candidacy of Ross Perot (18.9 percent): Bush (father) would almost surely have beaten Clinton head-to-head.

And in 2000 George W. Bush (47.9 percent) won with a bare majority of 271 Electoral College votes against Al Gore (48.4 percent) because of the candidacy of Ralph Nader. Bush's lead of a mere 537 (out of nearly 6 million) votes in Florida would have easily been erased if the 97,000 who voted for Nader could have expressed their preference for Gore.

Why does this happen? Because, as Lippmann suggested, MV does not permit voters to express their opinions fully.

In 1912 it was impossible for a Roosevelt voter to express a preference for Taft over Wilson, or a Taft voter to express a preference for Roosevelt over Wilson. Similarly, it was impossible for voters to express their preference for Bush (father) and Perot over Clinton in 1992, or for Nader voters in Florida to express their preference for Gore rather than Bush (son) in 2000. Had they been able to express their opinions of the candidates more accurately, the outcomes would have been different.

MV, as old as the hills, is merely a mechanism that has been accepted by force of habit. As Thomas Paine wrote in 1776 in "Common Sense"—"the most incendiary and popular pamphlet of the entire revolutionary era":

After the 2016 election, protesters urged the electors to vote their conscience—meaning anyone other than Donald Trump—rather than their party.

A long habit of not thinking a thing wrong gives it a superficial appearance of being right.

Majority voting is such a thing. It is thought to be democratic, but isn't, as these examples (and many others) show.

Ranked Voting's Failures

Some reformers advocate another mechanism, "ranked voting" (RV). Instead of choosing one among the candidates the voter lists them all from their most to their least preferred. This 18th-century idea (from the French mathematician and political scientist Jean-Charles de Borda) is a better scheme for voters to express themselves—and so it must have seemed to the narrow majority of 51.99 percent of Maine's voters who adopted one version of the possible methods based on RV, Ranked Choice Voting, in a statewide vote on November 8.

However, I argue that they were sold a bill of goods: RV's drawbacks completely disqualify it.

First and foremost, RV is far from permitting an adequate expression of the voters' opinions. A voter cannot reject all candidates, cannot consider two candidates equally good and cannot express strong versus lukewarm support (or rejection).

Furthermore, when RV has actually been used by juries in such competitions as figure skating, gymnastics and diving, its results have sometimes been so wildly peculiar that increasingly it has been abandoned in favor of methods that ask judges to evaluate competitors instead of ranking them. Figure skating juries' rules, for example, made the change in response to the 2002 winter Olympic scandal in pairs figure skating.

Majority Judgment

My colleague, Rida Laraki, and I have developed a new method of voting, majority judgment (MJ), which avoids the drawbacks of MV and RV.

MJ asks voters a simple and natural question such as that recently posed by the Pew Research Center: "What kind of president do you think each of the following would be—a great, good, average, poor or terrible president?" In its last national survey of registered voters

How voters judged the candidates, by percent					

Candidate	Great President	Good President	Average President	Poor President	Terrible President
Hillary Clinton	8	27	20	11	34
Donald Trump	9	18	16	11	46

Source: Pew Research Center

(Oct. 20-25) Pew reported the results in the above table (here adjusted to sum to 100 percent).

All one needs to do is look at the evaluations of the two candidates in the table above to conclude that Clinton is better evaluated than Trump.

But what exactly is the majority opinion?

Clinton would be an Average President because in a majority vote between Average and any other "grade," it wins. This is most easily seen by noting that a majority of 8%+27%+20%=55% believes she would be at least Average—so Average defeats any lower grade—and a majority of 20%+11%+34%=65% that she would be at most Average—so Average defeats any higher grade. It suffices to start from each end of the spectrum adding percentages until a majority is reached; in practice the sums from both directions will always reach a majority at the same grade.

Similarly, a majority believes Trump would be a Poor President because 54 percent believes he would be at least Poor and 57 percent that he would be at most Poor. With these evaluations majority judgment elects Clinton since the majority evaluates her above Trump.

MJ simply uses the majority principle—the idea that the majority can represent the whole—to deduce the electorate's evaluation of every candidate, called their majority-grades, instead of using it to compare the number of votes each candidate receives.

No system is perfect. But majority judgment is far superior to any other known system. Here's why:

FAST FACT

Common Sense author Thomas Paine believed government was a malevolent force and had much more faith in society.

- It is easier and more natural for voters since grading is familiar since school days;
- It obtains more information from voters and puts more confidence in them by permitting them to express their opinions accurately;
- It gives more information about the standing of candidates in the eyes of the public—had Clinton won she would have known her standing: Average;
- Most importantly, it elects the candidate highest in the esteem of the electorate.

What Happened This Year?

Pew Research—without realizing that their question serves as the basis of a method of voting—posed exactly the same question this year in January, March and August as well as late October.

In every case the majority evaluated Clinton an Average President and Trump a Poor President; moreover, their respective grades remained remarkably similar over all four polls, suggesting that despite all the hoopla—emails, sexism, racism, walls, FBI, secret speeches, jail and so much more – the electorate's opinions concerning the two candidates remained very much the same throughout the year.

And yet Trump beat Clinton. Why? MV denied voters the right to express their opinions adequately in the state face-to-face encounters.

U.S. voters were in revolt, determined to show their exasperation with politicians. But how, with the majority vote, could they express this disgust other than by voting for Trump?

With majority judgment some of them would surely have rated Clinton as Poor or Terrible to make the point, but Trump as Poor or Terrible as well, exactly as the Pew survey shows.

This could well have been the case in each of several states where their total votes were close such as Florida (a difference of 1.3 percent in their vote totals), Michigan (a difference of 0.3 percent), Wisconsin (a difference of 0.8 percent) and Pennsylvania (a difference of 1.1 percent). With MJ the result would then have been much closer to a true expression of voters' opinions and so of the popular will: 307 Electoral College votes for Clinton, 231 for Trump.

Well before the vote on Nov. 8 something else went wrong. Trump and Clinton should not have been the victors in the Republican and Democratic primaries—they are, after all, generally considered to be the least popular candidates of recent history. But the primaries were decided by majority vote as well. Had the primaries used majority judgment, the general election would have pitted Bernie Sanders against John Kasich.

Imagine how different the country and the world would feel today—and be tomorrow—had they been the candidates!

The time has come to replace the obviously undemocratic mechanism of the majority vote by a method that captures the true will of the electorate: majority judgment.

EVALUATING THE AUTHOR'S ARGUMENTS:

In this viewpoint, author Dale R. Durran uses a mathematical approach to solve his perceived problem of rigged presidential elections. How is this different from some of the other viewpoints you've read so far?

Viewpoint

5

Voting Matters to Many for a Variety of Reasons

Christopher Munsey

"There are two kinds of voters: Election-specific voters, who are motivated by a particular candidate or issue, and habitual voters, who consistently show up to vote in every election."

In the following excerpted viewpoint, Christopher Munsey contends that voting still matters to many individuals. Despite many factors that might turn us away from the polls, including time invested, inconvenience, and perceived futility, we overwhelmingly exercise our right. Given the relatively light weight of our individual vote, the fact that citizens show up to cast votes in elections is irrational, the author notes. So why do we bother? Munsey provides documentation from social psychologists, political scientists, and researchers citing various reasons why people vote. Munsey is on the staff of the American Psychological Association's *Monitor on Psychology*.

AS YOU READ, CONSIDER THE FOLLOWING QUESTIONS:

1. According to some research, which people tend not to vote?
2. What is the voter's illusion, according to the author?
3. What was significant in the study with mailed communication about an election?

©2017 by American Psychological Assocation. Reproduced with permission. Munsey, C. (2008, June)."Why Do We Vote?"Monitor on Psychology, 39(6). Retrieved from http://www.apa.org/monitor/2008/06/vote. aspx. No further reproduction or distribution is permitted without written permission from the American Psychological Association.

Voting is personally costly. It takes time to register and to learn about the candidates' views. On election day, you may need to leave work, stand in long lines or slog through harsh weather, knowing all the while that the chances your individual vote will make a difference among the thousands, or millions cast, are pretty much zero.

"The probability that I'll be the deciding vote in the 2008 presidential election is much smaller then the chance that I'll get hit by a car on the way to the polls," says Florida Atlantic University's Kevin Lanning, PhD, paraphrasing an observation made by the late University of Minnesota psychologist Paul E. Meehl.

"If we look at it in those terms alone, it appears to be irrational," Lanning says.

So Why Do We Bother?

Psychologists and political scientists have many theories. Some see voting as a form of altruism, or as a habitual behavior cued by yard signs and political ads. Others say voting may be a form of egocentrism, noting that some Americans appear to believe that because they are voting, people similar to them who favor the same candidate or party will probably vote, too, a psychological mechanism called the "voter's illusion."

Self-expression is likely to play a role as well, posits Lanning, who watches voting behavior as a poll worker in Palm Beach County, Fla. In a 2002 election, for example, he saw an ex-felon who repeatedly tried to vote. The man stood in line for an hour with his young children in tow and was turned away twice before voting officials verified that his voting rights had been restored.

"It mattered enough for him to go back and so the question is why?" Lanning says.

Looking back on the man's persistence, Lanning sees his determination to vote as an affirmative act that underscores his membership in the larger group, he says.

"We can think of voting as an expression of the self-concept," he says. "If I'm an American, and Americans vote, then the act of voting is an expression of who I am."

Despite voter apathy, the notion of voting as civic duty has been instilled in most Americans.

The Social Factors

Some research suggests that people are motivated to vote because they want to "fit in." Bruce Meglino, PhD, of the University of South Carolina's Moore School of Business, for example, sees voting as an example of a behavior included in social admonitions—things people are supposed to do—such as working hard when no one's watching or helping a stranger they'll never see again. Given that voting is an activity with more costs than benefits for the individual, Meglino thinks that highly rationally self-interested people probably don't bother to vote.

Research by Richard Jankowski, PhD, chair of the political science department at State University of New York, Fredonia, supports the role of altruism in voting. Looking back at questions posed in the American National Election Study's 1995 pilot study, Jankowski found that respondents who agreed with altruistic statements were more likely to have voted in 1994 elections.

"I found very strong evidence that people who vote tend to be highly altruistic, and people who don't vote tend to be much more self-interested," says Jankowski, who published his findings in *Rationality and Society* (Vol. 19, No. 1).

[...]

Some people, of course, vote because they believe their vote will make a difference, according to a study published by Melissa Acevedo, PhD, of Westchester Community College, and Joachim Krueger, PhD, of Brown University, in *Political Psychology* (Vol. 25, No.1).

"Basically, people just think their vote makes a difference, and have this mistaken belief even though statistically it's not the case," Acevedo says.

In their study, they proposed two possible projections that people make before an election that make it more likely that they'll vote: They vote, and their candidate wins, or They abstain, and their candidate loses.

Building on an idea first proposed by the late Amos Tversky, PhD, and George Quattrone, PhD, in 1984, Acevedo and Krueger think that voters might be acting on two egocentric mechanisms: One, the "voter's illusion," projects their own behavior to people similar to themselves likely to support the same candidate; the other allows them a route to believe that their individual votes can affect the outcome by forecasting what might happen if they don't vote.

[...]

Those behaviors support the contention that people believe their votes can make a difference on electoral outcomes, Krueger says.

[...]

Habits and Norms

But voting may be just plain habit for some people, according to Wendy Wood, PhD, a social psychologist at Duke University and co-director of the Social Science Research Institute. She worked with political scientists John Aldrich and Jacob Montgomery at Duke examining American National Election Study survey data in 10 midterm and presidential elections between 1958 and 2002. Her research suggests there are two kinds of voters: Election-specific voters, who are motivated by a particular candidate or issue, and habitual voters, who consistently show up to vote in every election. Habitual voters are much more likely to have lived at the same address over several elections and possess a "stable context" for voting. Voting by habit may be activated by such

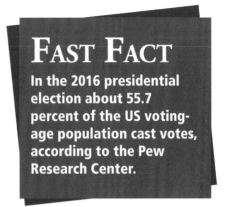

FAST FACT

In the 2016 presidential election about 55.7 percent of the US voting-age population cast votes, according to the Pew Research Center.

election cues as neighbors talking about politics or candidate signs posted in front yards, Wood says. (That's not to say they haven't carefully considered the issues: "You could show up habitually, but vote in a thoughtful way," Wood says.)

Less-habitual voters may vote due to social pressure, a significant factor in many people's decision to vote, according to Yale political scientist Donald Green, whose research shows the influence of one's peers: He conducted an experiment involving 180,000 Michigan households for the 2006 primary elections. About half of the group was the control group, and did not receive any mailed communication. The other half was divided into four groups, each targeted with a different mailing. People in the first group got a letter reminding them of the importance of doing their civic duty and voting. The second group received the same message, but they were also told that voting records were public records, and that their turnout was being studied. The third group got a letter listing whether or not they had voted in the last two elections, and were told that after the election, another letter would be sent to them indicating whether they voted in the upcoming election. The fourth group received a letter listing whether their neighbors had voted in the previous two elections, and told them that after the election, another letter would be sent out to them and their neighbors with a check mark next to their names indicating whether or not they had voted.

Among that fourth group, turnout rose by 8.1 percent in the primary, an effect Green described as "explosively large" compared with what's historically achieved in "get out the vote" mailings. Turnout rose by almost 4.9 percent in the group shown their own voting records and by 2.5 percent among the group told that their voting records were being studied, according to results published in the *American Political Science Review* (Vol. 102, No. 1).

Turnout in the control group was 29.7 percent, while turnout in the first group reminded of their civic duty to vote was 1.8 percentage points higher.

"Feeling obliged to comply with a social norm is indeed a powerful force," he says.

Such studies are important, notes Lanning, because they can give clues as to how to boost voter turnout among traditionally marginalized groups. If instead, people become convinced that elections aren't fair and that their participation doesn't matter, rule by the many can give way to the tyranny of the few, Lanning says.

"America is a great country, and we're great because people from so many different backgrounds can and do participate," he notes. "That greatness is at risk when significant groups, in significant numbers, don't participate as they could."

EVALUATING THE AUTHOR'S ARGUMENTS:

In this viewpoint Christopher Munsey cites studies that show the reasons why many individuals vote. If this is true, why do you suppose that there is rather low voter turnout for elections?

Chapter 3

Is There a Better Way to Determine Presidential Elections?

Many discouraged voters are calling for reforms to the election process.

The Electoral College Conflicts with the Popular Vote

"The very nature of the way the U.S. picks its presidents tends to create a disconnect between the outcome in the Electoral College and the popular vote."

Drew DeSilver

In the following viewpoint, Drew DeSilver argues that there is a mismatch between the Electoral College and the popular vote. DeSilver contends that this has happened five times in US history and that in some elections the margin of victory can be large or it can be small. The author also mentions the impactful record number of so-called faithless electors in the 2016 election. These are electors who cast their ballots for someone other than the official nominee of the party they're pledged to represent. DeSilver is a senior writer for the Pew Research Center.

AS YOU READ, CONSIDER THE FOLLOWING QUESTIONS:

1. According to the author, how did Donald Trump win the White House but lose the popular vote?
2. In what election was the disparity between the Electoral College and the popular vote the largest, as stated in the viewpoint?
3. What is the EV inflation factor as explained by the author?

"Trump's Victory Another Example of How Electoral College Wins are Bigger Than Popular Vote Ones," by Drew DeSilver, Pew Research Center, December 20, 2016. Reprinted by permission.

While nearly three million more people voted for Hillary Clinton than Donald Trump, Clinton found herself making a concession speech shortly after the election.

For the fifth time in U.S. history, and the second time this century, a presidential candidate has won the White House while losing the popular vote.

In this week's Electoral College balloting, Donald Trump won 304 electoral votes to Hillary Clinton's 227, with five Democratic and two Republican "faithless electors" voting for other people. That result was despite the fact that Clinton received nearly 2.9 million more popular votes than Trump in November's election, according to Pew Research Center's tabulation of state election results. Our tally shows Clinton won 65.8 million votes (48.25%) to almost 63 million (46.15%) for Trump, with minor-party and independent candidates taking the rest.

This mismatch between the electoral and popular votes came about because Trump won several large states (such as Florida, Pennsylvania and Wisconsin) by very narrow margins, gaining all their electoral votes in the process, even as Clinton claimed other large states (such as California, Illinois and New York) by much wider margins. Trump's share of the popular vote, in fact, was the seventh-smallest winning percentage since 1828, when presidential campaigns began to resemble those of today.

In fact, the very nature of the way the U.S. picks its presidents tends to create a disconnect between the outcome in the Electoral College and the popular vote. The last time a popular-vote loser won the presidency in the Electoral College was, of course, in 2000, when George W. Bush edged out Al Gore 271-266 despite Gore winning some 537,000 more popular votes nationwide. The other electoral-popular vote mismatches came in 1876 and 1888; in all four instances the Democratic nominee ended up the loser. (In the 1824 election, which was contested between rival factions of the old Democratic-Republican Party, Andrew Jackson won a plurality of the popular and electoral vote, but because he was short of an Electoral College majority the election was thrown to the House of Representatives, which chose runner-up John Quincy Adams.)

Even in the vast majority of U.S. elections, in which the same candidate won both the popular and the electoral vote, the system usually makes the winner's victory margin in the former a lot wider than in the latter. In 2012, for example, Barack Obama won 51% of the nationwide popular vote but nearly 62% of the electoral votes, or 332 out of 538.

Looking back at all presidential elections since 1828, the winner's electoral vote share has, on average, been 1.36 times his popular vote share—what we'll call the electoral vote (EV) inflation factor. Trump's EV inflation factor, based on his winning 56.5% of the electoral votes (304 out of 538) is 1.22, similar to Obama's in 2012 (1.21).

A quick Electoral College refresher: The 538 electors allocated (mainly by population) among the 50 states and the District of Columbia actually choose the president and vice president, with a majority of electoral votes (i.e., 270) needed for an outright win. All but two states use a plurality winner-take-all system to pick their presidential electors—whoever receives the most votes in a state wins all of its electoral votes, even if he or she got less than a majority of the popular vote. (Maine and Nebraska award some of their electoral votes by congressional district rather than statewide; that enabled

Trump to win one of Maine's four electoral votes, for the state's 2nd District, even though Clinton won the state overall.)

The biggest disparity between the winning electoral and popular votes, with an EV inflation factor of 1.96, came in 1912 in the four-way slugfest between Democrat Woodrow Wilson, Republican incumbent William Howard Taft, Progressive Theodore Roosevelt (who had bolted from the Republicans) and Socialist Eugene V. Debs. Wilson won a whopping 82% of the electoral votes—435 out of 531—with less than 42% of the overall popular vote. (In fact, Wilson won popular vote majorities in only 11 of the 40 states he carried – all in what was then the solidly Democratic South.)

The next biggest gap was the 1980 "Reagan landslide." In that three-way contest, Ronald Reagan took just under 51% of the popular vote, to Jimmy Carter's 41% and independent John Anderson's 6.6%. But Reagan soared past Carter in the Electoral College: 489 electoral votes (91% of the total) to 49, for an EV inflation factor of 1.79.

Many of the elections with the most-inflated electoral votes featured prominent third-party candidates, who served to hold down the winners' popular vote share without being significant Electoral College players themselves. On the other hand, when the two major-party nominees ran fairly evenly and there were no notable independents or third parties, the Electoral College vote has tended to be much closer to the popular tally. In 2004, for instance, incumbent Bush won a second term with just under 51% of the popular vote and 53% of the electoral votes (286 out of 538).

A notable feature of the 2016 Electoral College vote was the record number of so-called "faithless electors"—electors who cast their ballots for someone other than the official nominee of the party they're pledged to represent. The five Democratic electors who voted

FAST FACT

According to state election results tabulated by the Pew Research Center, Hillary Clinton racked up nearly three million more popular votes than Donald Trump.

for people other than Clinton included three from Washington State who chose Colin Powell and another who chose Yankton Sioux tribal elder Faith Spotted Eagle, and one from Hawaii who voted for Vermont Sen. Bernie Sanders, Clinton's rival in the primaries. In addition, the two Texas electors who spurned Trump voted instead for Ohio Gov. John Kasich (whom Trump had defeated in the primaries) and former U.S. Rep. Ron Paul.

EVALUATING THE AUTHOR'S ARGUMENTS:

In this viewpoint Drew DeSilver presents statistics outlining the gap between Electoral College wins versus popular vote totals. In view of this, do you think that DeSilver would favor having only two candidates on the presidential ticket?

Reject the National Popular Vote Plan

"By making 'every vote count' [the National Popular Vote] would incentivize voter fraud in every city and state."

Kevin Kane

In the following viewpoint, written before the 2012 presidential election but still relevant today, Kevin Kane argues that the National Popular Vote plan should be rejected. While many believe the National Popular Vote would be a worthy replacement to our flawed Electoral College system, Kane believes that having state electors choose the candidate with the most nationwide votes is a dangerous idea. The author makes his case in six clear points. Kane clearly outlines reasons why Louisiana's House of Representatives would be wrong to consider replacing the Electoral College system. Kane was the president and founder of the Pelican Institute for Public Policy.

AS YOU READ, CONSIDER THE FOLLOWING QUESTIONS:
1. According to the author, how would the National Popular Vote (NPV) encourage fraud?
2. How will the NPV affect smaller states, according to the author?
3. What is a constitutional "workaround" as explained in the viewpoint?

"Six Reasons to Reject National Popular Vote," by Kevin Kane, The Pelican Post, May 4, 2012. Reprinted by permission.

On Monday, Louisiana's House of Representatives is expected to vote on HB 1095. This bill would make Louisiana party to the National Popular Vote (NPV) "compact" whereby state electors would pledge to cast their votes to the presidential candidate receiving the most votes nationwide, regardless of the results in Louisiana. Here are six reasons why legislators should reject this attempt to jettison our electoral system:

1. Louisiana voters should decide who receives Louisiana's electoral votes.

Our state will likely vote overwhelmingly for the Republican challenger to Barack Obama in November. But NPV could force our electors to disregard the wishes of the citizens they represent and vote instead for President Obama. Louisianans should decide where their electoral votes go, not voters in New York, Illinois or California.

2. National elections will encourage widespread voter fraud and increase the likelihood of nationwide recounts.

Supporters of NPV claim that controversial recounts like Florida in 2000 would be a thing of the past. This is untrue. In fact, by making "every vote count" NPV would incentivize voter fraud in every city and state. Political machines would swing into action and squeeze every possible vote out of each district in hopes of swinging a national election. Further, a competitive election would produce a replay of Florida 2000, but on a national scale. Recounts would take place across the United States, along with endless litigation and doubts about the legitimacy of the eventual winner.

3. State autonomy will be threatened as elections are nationalized.

While a system with state-by-state guidelines for voter eligibility, candidate qualification and electoral selection has drawbacks, it is consistent with our respect for state sovereignty. This tradition of state

How can we make sure the right candidate makes it to the White House?

autonomy will be threatened as elections are nationalized and pressure for uniform standards grows. Standards for voter eligibility or certifying ballots will be seen as national rather than state questions and pressure will mount for a universal approach requiring central control. It will become one more transfer of power from the states to the federal government. This is not a development most Louisianans would support.

4. Smaller states like Louisiana will not benefit because national campaigns will focus on major media markets.

While NPV supporters claim that states like Louisiana will become more relevant to national campaigns, in fact the candidates will logically focus on major media markets across the country. New York, Chicago, Dallas and Los Angeles might benefit from this change but

FAST FACT

According to the
National Archives there
have been seven hundred
proposals to change the
Electoral College in the
last two hundred years.

Louisiana would not. It is a fact that the significance of individual states will wax and wane over the years. Louisiana was an important swing state in the recent past and will be one again someday. Doing away with our system will not make Louisiana a permanent player on the national stage.

5. Candidates and officeholders will not lose their ability to "buy votes" through policy initiatives.

Supporters of NPV argue that national elections will prevent candidates from targeting swing states with policy "giveaways". They cite George W. Bush's support for expanded Medicare benefits, which was popular in Florida, as an example. But in a national election candidates will still attempt to win over demographic groups, and NPV could encourage them to become even more aggressive as they seek to capture support from larger segments of the population. The phenomenon of "buying votes" is a feature of our democracy that cannot be legislated out of existence. NPV will not only fail to accomplish this goal, it could make things worse.

6. Amending the Constitution is the appropriate method for changing our electoral system.

Legislators understand that policy questions must be addressed in a Constitutional manner. Those who believe that NPV offers a better way to elect a president should still reject this bill because it seeks to evade the amendment process. While state compacts serve legitimate purposes, abolishing our system of selecting presidents is not one of them. This is an attempt at a Constitutional "workaround" and should be rejected. The proper approach is to seek to amend the Constitution. This is not easy, but if the arguments for NPV are persuasive its supporters should be willing to take up this challenge rather than relying on gimmicks.

Conclusion

Legislators contemplating support for this bill should take counsel from President John F. Kennedy: "Don't ever take a fence down until you know the reason why it was put up." Our Founding Founders strategically placed fences in an effort to balance power among the branches of federal government and the states. This balance has served our nation well and it should not be cast aside.

Our institutions and systems are not perfect. They are political creations and reflect the conflicts and compromises inherent in such endeavors. But the current system of electing a president is consistent with the values and priorities of our Founders and remains the best way to choose a leader for this large and diverse nation. Louisiana legislators should reject NPV and vote no on HB 1095.

EVALUATING THE AUTHOR'S ARGUMENTS:

In this viewpoint Kevin Kane proposes an argument for rejecting the National Popular Vote plan. Explain the metaphor used by President John F. Kennedy and how it supports Kane's argument.

States Should Adopt the National Popular Vote Plan

"Candidates for our one national office should have incentives to speak to everyone, and all Americans should have the power to hold their president accountable."

Rob Richie

In the following viewpoint Rob Richie contends that the National Popular Vote should be put into effect, thereby changing the presidential election system. Richie contends that the Electoral College is disliked and charges it with being "a broken system." Richie outlines the benefits of the NPV and analyzes popular objections to the plan. Richie is executive director of FairVote, a nonpartisan organization that champions electoral reforms. In addition to coauthoring *Every Vote Equal,* his work has appeared in various media outlets.

AS YOU READ, CONSIDER THE FOLLOWING QUESTIONS:

1. What will happen if the Electoral College system is left unchanged, according to the author?
2. How do swing states matter, according to the author?
3. What is one way to address objections to the NPV, as stated in this viewpoint?

"Why States Should Adopt the National Popular Vote Plan for President," by Rob Richie, The San Diego Union-Tribune, May 17, 2009. Reprinted by permission.

The Electoral College is understandably the single-most disliked feature of the American Constitution.

As implemented by states today, it is an antiquated anachronism that violates fundamental principles of representative democracy. It weights votes differently based on where they are cast, makes the national popular vote irrelevant and creates opportunities for partisans to game the system through changing the rules governing how votes are counted and how electoral votes are allocated. Left unchanged, our Electoral College system promises to deepen political inequality, with a damaging impact on small states, young voters, urban America, people of color and all the Americans living outside swing states.

A Broken System

Consider these facts about our broken system from FairVote's 2009 edition of Presidential Election Inequality:

- Of 300 major-party presidential campaign events tracked by The Washington Post between Sept. 5 and Nov. 4, 2008, 57 percent took place in the four large swing states of Ohio, Florida, Pennsylvania and Virginia. As tracked by CNN from Sept. 24 through Election Day, 55 percent of all presidential campaign ads aired in those same four states.
- More than 98 percent of all campaign events and all campaign spending in the fall took place in 15 states that collectively represent only 37 percent of the nation's eligible voter population, effectively sidelining two-thirds of all Americans.
- Voter turnout in those 15 states was 6 percent higher than the rest of the country. In 2004, young eligible voters under 30 were a third more likely to vote in the 10 closest states, and all of the 10 states with the greatest rate of decline in youth turnout since 1972 were spectator states.
- According to one of its key strategists, Matthew Dowd, George Bush's campaign for re-election did not poll a single person who lived outside one of 18 potential battleground states for the final 30 months of the campaign.

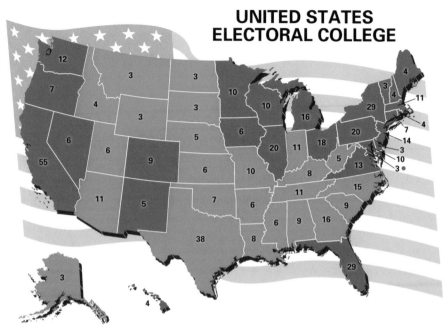

UNITED STATES ELECTORAL COLLEGE

This map illustrates the number of electoral votes allotted to each state. A candidate needs more than half, or 270, to win.

Trends are making this inequality worse. Consider that:

- In 1960, 24 states with a total of 319 electoral votes were swing states—meaning states within a 47 percent-53 percent partisanship band in a nationally even year. Using this same swing state definition, in 2008 there were only nine swing states with a total of 115 electoral votes.

- In trends partly obscured by Barack Obama's 7 percent victory in the national popular vote, four recent battleground states (Michigan, Wisconsin, New Mexico and Missouri) trended to being spectator status in a future election in which the major-party vote was evenly divided. Only one state (Indiana) moved from noncompetitive status to being a potential battleground.

- In 1960, nine states with a total of 64 electoral votes were considered firm "spectator" states, with a partisanship of more than 58 percent for one party. In 2008, this number was 26 states with 277 electoral votes.

- In the 1976 presidential election, 73 percent of African-Americans were in a classic swing-voter position: they lived in highly competitive states (won by less than 5 percent) in which African-Americans were at least 5 percent of the population. By 2000, that percentage of potential African American swing voters had declined to just 17 percent.
- The average difference in partisanship between the 10 most Republican and 10 most Democratic states has widened from 16 percent in 1988 to 27 percent in 2004 and 29 percent in 2008—a gulf between states that can only be bridged in presidential elections by making every vote equal.

An Alternative Plan

Instead of this debased method of election, every American voter should have equal power to hold their president accountable through a national popular vote for president. With popular vote elections governing how we elect every governor and member of Congress, we know what such elections look like. As the vote totals rise on election night, voters know that their votes are counted on an equal basis with everyone else and that, when all the counting is done, the candidate with the most votes will win.

The National Popular Vote plan provides our best opportunity to achieve this goal. Laid out in detail at nationalpopularvote.com, the plan is based on two powers granted to states under the Constitution. First, states have exclusive power to decide how to allocate electoral votes—one characterized by the Supreme Court as "supreme" and "plenary."

Initially, few states awarded all electoral votes to the statewide vote winner—several, in fact, didn't even hold popular elections. It was not until Andrew Jackson's presidency that the winner-take-all unit rule became the norm, driven by states' partisan parochial incentives to give as many votes as possible to one candidate. The unit rule isn't in the Constitution, wasn't intended by the framers of our Constitution and is most certainly not in the best interests of our nation.

Second, states have the constitutionally protected power to enter into formal, binding agreements. There are hundreds of examples, including the Port Authority and the Colorado River Compact.

Fewer than 1,000 words, the National Popular Vote compact establishes that participating states will award all of their electoral votes to the slate of the candidate who wins the national popular vote in all 50 states and the District of Columbia. It is activated if—and only if—the participating states collectively have a majority of votes in the Electoral College.

States enter the compact one by one, passing a statute through regular legislative channels. If by July 2012, states adopting the compact collectively have a majority of electoral votes (currently 270 of 538), the agreement is set in stone for the year, and the White House is guaranteed to the candidate who wins the popular vote. Electoral votes would still elect the president and the total number of electoral votes won by a candidate might vary based on which states are in the compact, but no one would focus on electoral vote margins. All attention before and after the election would be on the popular vote. Gone would be the red-blue maps on election night and the early projections of winners while Western states are still voting. Every voter would count the same, whether it is cast in Maine, Alaska, Texas or Florida.

NPV Plan Advances

Since the plan's launch by National Popular Vote in 2006, it has passed into law in Hawaii, Illinois, Maryland, New Jersey and Washington. Bills have been introduced in 48 states and earned the votes or sponsorship of more than 1,700 legislators. Endorsers include *The New York Times*, *Los Angeles Times*, Common Cause, the NAACP, columnists E.J Dionne and Hendrik Hertzberg and former members of Congress Tom Campbell, R-Calif., Jake Garn, R-Utah, John Anderson, R-Ill., and Birch Bayh, D-Ind.

With media interest beginning to rise, the proposal's popularity will keep growing. In polls taken by National Popular Vote since the 2008 elections, the number of citizens supporting a national popular vote for president reflects landslide support in a full range of states, including 68 percent in Colorado, 78 percent in Florida, 75 percent in Iowa, 73 percent in Michigan, 69 percent in New Hampshire, 72 percent in Nevada, 74 percent in North Carolina and 78 percent in Pennsylvania.

The last time the nation had a similar focus on reforming the Electoral College was in 1969-70, after several congressional hearings, a controversial election in 1960 and concerns about the impact of independent candidate George Wallace on the 1968 election. National support for a national popular vote reached 80 percent in Gallup polls, and a proposed constitutional amendment to abolish the Electoral College won the votes of 81 percent of U.S. House members, including future Presidents Gerald Ford and George H.W. Bush. It faltered in the Senate only because of parliamentary procedures denying majority support for change.

The case for reform is even stronger today. In the 1960s, far more states were contested, and there was more fluctuation in voting patterns. We are better prepared for a national popular vote, with more uniform voting standards and patterns of participation.

Addressing Objections

Objections to the NPV plan generally fall into three categories: (1) defense of the current Electoral College system, with a kind of magical thinking that the success of the United States is connected to the Electoral College; (2) belief that the "right way" to replace the current system is by amending the Constitution; (3) support for alternative reform approaches.

Defenders of the current Electoral College present a grab-bag of arguments. They suggest fairer elections for president might undermine federalism despite the fact that the NPV plan doesn't diminish state powers under the Constitution or have any impact on the U.S. Senate. They argue that the United States in the 21st century is incapable of fairly administering close popular vote elections, despite the examples of large states such as Texas and California and large nations such as Brazil. They warn that third parties would start having a much bigger impact despite the lack of evidence from the thousands of statewide popular vote elections for governor and U.S. Senate. They argue that candidates would only spend time in big population states and cities even though the numbers show such a strategy would be a losing formula.

FAST FACT

For the 2016 election, Politico identified eleven states as battleground or swing states.

Those touting a constitutional amendment present a false choice, as many National Popular Vote advocates support both it and amendment strategies. Certainly the winner-take-all unit rule system used by most states is not "more constitutional" than the National Popular Vote plan; it's just the status quo that was adopted by the 1830s and one that as implemented today would shock our Founders, who wanted all states to have a meaningful role in presidential elections. States nearly always have taken the lead in advancing a more representative democracy, including in expanding suffrage rights to women and people without property and establishing popular election of U.S. senators. Even if the compact is established by state laws rather than federal law, Congress would have the power to establish rules to resolve any administrative concerns, such as how to conduct recounts.

Alternate reform approaches can have zealous advocates, but are either dead in the water politically or unlikely to meet the goals of voter equality and majority rule.

As one example, FairVote's review of allocating electoral votes by congressional district shows that if established nationally, it would have an extreme partisan bias. Both congressional district allocation and proportional allocation of electors within states would keep many states sidelined—and trying to pass these reforms state by state is problematic and prone to partisan gaming of the national rules.

Other novel approaches perhaps could be tried for local and state offices, but for presidential elections a straight-up one person-one vote election is the only reform that is tested and meets voters' expectation of transparency and popularity.

With a national popular vote, presidential campaigns would seek votes everywhere in a true 50-state effort. Every vote—in every corner of every state—would be equal. Americans could get involved in presidential campaigns in their own communities.

The bottom line is that candidates for our one national office should have incentives to speak to everyone, and all Americans should have the power to hold their president accountable. Only a national popular vote will do. Now, with the National Popular Vote campaign, we have a sensible road map for change.

EVALUATING THE AUTHOR'S ARGUMENTS:

In this viewpoint Rob Richie supports the adoption of the National Popular Vote plan. Compare Richie's views and analysis to those of Kevin Kane in the previous viewpoint.

Improved Civic Instruction in School Leads to Informed Voting

"Significant gaps remain in one of the most basic forms of civic participation— voter turnout."

Abby Kiesa and Peter Levine

In the following viewpoint, Abby Kiesa and Peter Levine discuss and analyze civic education in America. The authors outline what they believe is a troubling issue— the low turnout of young voters and the equally low participation of young people in civic matters. The authors suggest that improved civic education would stem the tide of nonparticipation and increase voter turnout. Kiesa is the director of Impact at CIRCLE, a research center dedicated to youth education. Levine is associate dean for research of citizenship and public affairs at Tufts University.

AS YOU READ, CONSIDER THE FOLLOWING QUESTIONS:

1. According to the authors, what social movements have emerged over the last decade?
2. What problems do teachers have in teaching civics?
3. How could teachers improve civic education according to the authors?

"Why America Urgently Needs to Improve K-12 Civic Education," by Abby Kiesa and Peter Levine, The Conversation, October 30, 2016, https://theconversation.com/why-america-urgently-needs-to-improve-k-12-civic-education-66736?sa=google&sq=voter+turnout&sr=17. Licensed under CC BY ND 4.0 International.

Getting involved in political campaigns can engage young people in voting and elections.

The tone of this presidential election, often called "uncivil," has led many to call for an urgent improvement of civic education in America.

Civic education can teach citizens how to deliberate, even when they have political differences. It can enable citizens to find solutions to many problems such as school attendance, economic development or community safety.

For over a decade, we've worked as researchers investigating a wide range of questions related to youth civic participation. Over this period, we have observed how civic life has been transformed. New technologies emerged as well as new political and social movements, such as the Tea Party, Occupy Wall Street and the movement for black lives—all of which have changed civic life. Indeed, today's youth have a lot more opportunities to express their political views and take action through online platforms.

However, significant gaps remain in one of the most basic forms of civic participation—voter turnout. Only about 40–45 percent of 18-to-29-year-olds turned out to vote in the 2012 election, and gaps among youth remain a concern in 2016.

One big reason for these voting rates is in the way many public K-12 schools are teaching civics: Students may be learning about the mechanics of government, but they are not always required to learn the skills needed for civic participation. Teachers, meanwhile, have voiced concern that lessons about elections and politics will be perceived by some as partisan.

The Missing Young Voters

Currently, there are dramatic gaps among youth when it comes to voter turnout. The young people who regularly vote look like the youth population as a whole because youth do not vote at the same rates. Our analysis of state and federal voting data shows that young people without college experience remain underrepresented.

For example, in the 2012 election, 56 percent of youth with any college experience voted compared to only 29 percent of youth with no college experience. These young people between 18 and 29 make up 40 percent of the youth population.

The gap was just as large in the high turnout election of 2008, where 62 percent of youth with any college experience voted, compared to only 36 percent of youth with no college experience. Our analysis of census data suggests this trend is not new and this gap has existed for decades.

Why is Civic Participation of Youth So Low?

Civic education can not only increase youth voting, but in doing so also begin to close historic voting gaps. Our research shows, however, civic education itself remains a neglected area in in American schools.

Most states do not consider civic education as a vital part of student learning. While social studies is part of the curriculum in most states, reports from 2013 show only eight states assess students' civic performance.

The curriculum itself leaves much to be desired. Too often, in public schools, civic education is reduced to learning history and dry information about governmental processes. Students learn significantly more historical information – for instance, about wars and individual people – than skills that can teach them how to solve problems.

FAST FACT

According to a 2014 report by the US Department of Education, only 23 percent of eighth graders were proficient in civics.

Research into state social studies curriculum standards shows they often do not include learning in detail about modern parties and their ideologies. The results differ by state, but the general trends are striking. For example, this research indicates that "Democrat" and "Republican" are not often found in school curricula and only 10 states ask that students learn what these parties stand for.

It's difficult to understand how a young person would understand American politics without this ability to differentiate.

Other Challenges

In addition, schools don't help students connect their learning to practice. It is students in wealthier schools, or who are on a "college track," who are more likely to find opportunities to learn about civic engagement through discussions or hands-on research that allows them to work on finding solutions to civic problems that they care about.

For example, a group of high school students in Chicago, after learning how to make their voices heard on civic issues, campaigned to have bus stop benches along major bus routes.

Another big challenge when it comes to civic education is public resistance to teaching anything remotely connected to electoral politics in public schools.

In a less controversial election (2012), teachers told us they believed that they would receive a pushback if they taught about politics and elections.

In a national survey of over 700 teachers we conducted during the spring after the 2012 election, more than one in four current teachers of US government or civics said that they would expect criticism from parents or other adults if they taught the election that had taken place that fall. Only one-third (38 percent) said they would get strong support from their district.

Concerns about introducing elections to classrooms are misplaced, since research has not found patterns of teachers influencing students' preferences in elections. We found in 2012 that taking civics didn't correlate with either partisanship or vote choice.

Improving Turnout

Existing research demonstrates that engaging youth in elections before they reach the age of 18 can increase the likelihood of voting. Classroom teaching practices where young people learn about current issues or can practice having conversations with different viewpoints involved can start to close these gaps.

These more active teaching practices allow youth to increase knowledge and develop skills, such as how to communicate effectively with someone with differing views. In turn, this can also build a young person's confidence in their own ability to participate. Knowledge alone is not enough to ensure future civic engagement.

Our research shows that classroom teaching practices were positively related to informed voting, the idea of voting with accurate knowledge about the democratic system and preferred candidates.

Additionally, preregistration laws, which allow 16- and 17-year-olds to preregister and then automatically join the voter rolls when they turn 18, boost turnout. Appearance on a list of registered voters means that these preregistered youth are more likely to be contacted by parties and interest groups that use lists of registered voters for outreach.

As a result, easing youth into civic participation, through preregistration and starting to experience structured civic participation in the classroom, can prove valuable to later engagement, like voting.

Voting is habit-forming. Closing gaps early by strengthening the connection between school civic education and civic participation could ensure that our electorate will more fully represent the U.S. population.

EVALUATING THE AUTHOR'S ARGUMENTS:

In this viewpoint Abby Kiesa and Peter Levine contend that low voter turnout among young people has its roots in poor civics education in school. Does your school offer civics education? How does this affect your knowledge and interest in participation in issues related to voting?

Viewpoint

5

To Effect Change, Reform the Presidential Primary System

"The presidential primary system as it exists today is a surprisingly new phenomenon, and it is hardly unreasonable to believe that it can and should be overhauled."

Maru Gonzalez

In the following viewpoint, Maru Gonzalez asserts that the presidential primary is the root of our flawed election system. The primary is relatively new and could be easily changed, compared to the Electoral College. The author presents five key reasons why she believes the presidential primary system should be reformed because it undermines democracy. However, she believes that reform is unlikely to happen because too many powerful people benefit from primaries. Gonzalez is a scholar, activist, and educator and is a frequent contributor to the Huffington Post.

AS YOU READ, CONSIDER THE FOLLOWING QUESTIONS:

1. Explain the author's meaning of the phrase "all votes are not created equal" when it comes to voting in primary elections.
2. What are the author's problems concerning delegates?
3. Should there be early voting states, according to the viewpoint?

"5 Reasons the Presidential Primary System Is in Need of Reform," by Maru Gonzalez, The Huffington Post, March 31, 2016. Reprinted by permission.

During the 2016 campaign season, the Republican Party featured a whopping seventeen primary candidates!

Every four years we see the same song and dance: a diverse mix of party elders, rising stars and professional agitators competing for their party's nomination to the highest political office our nation has to offer. And so begins a bizarre series of rituals that, in spite of quadrennial gripes from a few pundits and shared Facebook posts, we seem to accept as an engrained and sacred part of the democratic process.

But the presidential primary system as it exists today is a surprisingly new phenomenon, and it is hardly unreasonable to believe that it can and should be overhauled. Below are just a few reasons why that's exactly what needs to be done.

1. State-by-state discrepancies make the primary process imbalanced

Most states and territories hold primaries, which are organized and paid for by their respective state governments. The remaining states and territories opt for caucuses and party nominating conventions, where complicated rules and long processes mean voter turnout is often much lighter than in primaries. Some contests are open to all voters regardless of political affiliation, while others are solely intended for pledged party members. Such wide variation among states means that all votes are not created equal. Issues of accessibility and voter impact at the ballot box are directly contingent upon the rules that govern each state's primary process.

2. Delegate allocation is confusing—and undemocratic
The process by which delegates are allocated also varies by state and by party. On the Republican side, each state is granted leeway in determining how delegates are assigned. Many states allocate delegates on a winner-take-all or winner-take-most basis, a process that effectively undermines individual votes. In Texas, for example, the state party only awards delegates to candidates who meet a 20 percent threshold of the popular vote, which essentially rendered meaningless the over 500,000 votes (roughly 18 percent) cast for Rubio. On the Democratic side, candidates must acquire at least 15 percent of the state's popular vote in order to accrue pledged delegates, a policy that did not bode well for Clinton supporters in Vermont where she received just shy of 14 percent.

For Kasich supporters in Georgia (where he fell far short of the 20 percent threshold), they would have been just as well writing in Paul Coverdell, who despite his postmortem conditions will receive the same number of Georgian delegates as Kasich come July. Meanwhile, Donald Trump will arrive in Cleveland with about 43 percent of the pledged delegates awarded through March, despite only receiving 35 percent of the votes cast in that same time.

3. Closed primaries and caucuses discourage broad participation
On this point, there are clearly pros and cons to restricting primary participation to party members. As Rush Limbaugh's "Operation Chaos" illustrated in 2008, open primaries can persuade members

of another party to participate with the goal of disrupting the process rather than selecting a nominee on his or her merits. In the 2016 Michigan primary, some pundits prognosticated that many of Hillary Clinton's supporters may have crossed over to vote against Donald Trump. So clearly, political parties have a vested interest in keeping primaries closed to discourage agitation and maintain party loyalty.

FAST FACT

According to Bloomberg Politics, a presidential candidate becomes a party's nominee when he or she wins a majority of delegates. For Republicans, that means a majority of the 2,472 delegates, and for Democrats, a majority of 4,762.

Yet, should open primaries even be a question in a democratic contest? Shouldn't citizens, whose tax dollars fund primaries, be allowed to vote strategically in order to achieve a desired result? And why should only Democrats and Republicans have a say in deciding which candidates are most qualified to serve as commander in chief? By shutting out unaffiliated voters, states with closed primaries and caucuses see much lower participation, which is arguably worse for political parties whose ultimate success in the general election is based on high voter turnout.

4. Early states wield disproportionate amounts of power and do not reflect the broader electorate

The power of early states rests in their ability to create momentum for candidates. Yet the combined population of the first four primary states—Iowa, New Hampshire, Nevada and South Carolina — is a little more than 12 million people. That is less than one-third of the population of California alone, yet you don't see a lot of presidential hopefuls eating fried guava on a stick with voters in the suburbs of San Diego. That's because Californians don't vote until June 7, and in most recent cycles the parties have settled on nominees well before they get the chance to participate.

Further, the electorate in first states to vote hardly represent the diversity of the nation as a whole. According to the most recent census, 92.1 percent of Iowans identify as purely white. Compare that with the 36.3 percent nationwide who identify as anything other than white, and the discrepancy is glaring. In New Hampshire the gap is amazingly even wider, with an even 94 percent identifying as white and white alone.

5. Superdelegates are fundamentally undemocratic

Hilariously enough, the arguably undemocratic role of superdelegates—who are tasked with casting their votes for a candidate of their choosing at party conventions — only exist on the Democratic side. Despite the fact that their votes are not bound by the results of popular elections in their state, their votes weigh much more heavily than the votes of average citizens. While Bernie Sanders earned 15 pledged delegates to Hillary Clinton's nine in New Hampshire, six superdelegates have declared their support to Clinton, forcing an effective tie at the convention. If New Hampshire's two uncommitted superdelegates end up swinging into Clinton's camp, she will defeat Bernie Sanders on the floor despite losing the popular vote in that state by more than 20 percent.

While superdelegates are solely a byproduct of the DNC, Republicans have their own version of the "smoke-filled room": unbound delegates, or delegates who essentially become free agents if the candidate to whom they were bound suspends their campaign. And because there is no law barring unbound delegates from accepting bribes, they could theoretically sell their vote to the highest bidder on the convention floor.

All of this matters because the rules that govern presidential primaries serve the plutocrats and party elites, rather than the will of the people. Our current system fuels the 24-hour corporate media circus, forces (most) candidates into the pockets of special interests, disenfranchises voters, and perpetuates a two-part duopoly that undermines our democracy. Yet as long as the media and the two major parties stand to benefit from this process—and the public is willing to play along—we can continue to expect more of the same.

EVALUATING THE AUTHOR'S ARGUMENTS:

In this viewpoint Maru Gonzalez contends that the presidential primary system must be reformed so that a fundamental change will occur in America's democratic process. Is this the real problem with the election process in the United States? Support your opinion with facts from at least one other viewpoint from chapter three.

Facts About the Electoral College and the Popular Vote

Editor's note: These facts can be used in reports to add credibility when making important points or claims.

Facts About Federal Elections

- Presidential elections occur every four years in November. The election is on the Tuesday after the first Monday in November, or on the Tuesday between November 2 and November 8th.
- All eligible citizens vote for a ticket of candidates that includes a candidate for president and a candidate for vice president.
- Unless citizens in the US territories have official residency (live in) in a US state or the District of Columbia, they cannot vote in the presidential election.
- Voter turnout in the United States often lags behind many other nations (other members of the OECD, the Organization for Economic Cooperation and Development).
- Highest percentage of voting in the OECD members occurs in Belgium (about 87 percent), Sweden (about 82 percent), and Denmark (about 80 percent).
- Lowest ranking percentage of voting in the OECD occurs in Switzerland at less than 39 percent.
- Since 1870, African Americans have had the right to vote, set by the Fifteenth Amendment to the US Constitution.
- Since 1920, women have had the right to vote, set by the Nineteenth Amendment to the US Constitution.
- Since 1971, the minimum age to vote has been eighteen, which was set by the Twenty-Sixth Amendment to the US Constitution.
- Voter registration in the United States is an individual responsibility.
- In the 2016 presidential election about 55.7 percent of the US voting-age population cast votes according to the Pew Research Center.

Facts About the Electoral College

- The Electoral College was created in 1787 at the Constitutional Convention.
- The president and vice president of the United States are elected by the Electoral College.
- According to the US Constitution, each state has electors "equal to the whole Number of Senators and Representatives to which the State may be entitled in the Congress."
- Washington, DC, has the same number of electors it would have if it was a state and no more than the state with the least number of citizens.
- The presidential candidate with the majority of Electoral College votes and at least 270 wins the election.
- The Electoral College has 538 electors.
- Every state except for Nebraska and Maine award all of the electoral votes of the state to the candidate winning the popular vote of that state.
- The electoral votes in Maine and Nebraska are awarded to winner of congressional district voting, and the statewide popular vote winner receives two extra votes.
- When you vote for your candidate in the presidential election you are actually voting for your candidate's electors.
- The top three states with the most Electoral College votes are California, New York, and Texas.
- In December, the electors meet in their respective state capitols to cast their ballots for president and vice president.
- Each state's electoral votes are counted in a joint session of Congress before members of the House and Senate on the 6th of January in the year following the meeting of the electors.
- The president-elect takes the oath of office and is sworn in as president of the United States on January 20th in the year following the presidential election.
- Support for the Electoral College has risen from 35 percent in 2014 to 47 percent in 2016 according to a Gallup poll.

Facts About the Popular Vote

- In 2016, Senator Barbara Boxer proposed a bill for an amendment to the US Constitution that would abolish the Electoral College.
- The National Popular Vote Plan (NPV) is an interstate compact in which the member states agree to award their electoral votes to the candidate winning the national popular vote.
- The NPV has been enacted into law by eleven states, with a total of 165 electoral votes.
- The NPV will take effect when the number of electoral votes held by the enacting states equals 270.
- Some view the NPV as an "end-around" the US Constitution. They contend that to change the current voting system, the US Constitution would need to be amended. That requires a two-thirds vote by the House and Senate and additional support from three-fourths of state legislatures.

Organizations to Contact

The editors have compiled the following list of organizations concerned with the issues debated in this book. The descriptions are derived from materials provided by the organizations. All have publications or information available for interested readers. The list was compiled on the date of publication of the present volume; the information provided here may change. Be aware that many organizations take several weeks or longer to respond to inquiries, so allow as much time as possible for the receipt of requested materials.

Cato Institute
1000 Massachusetts Avenue NW
Washington, DC 20001
(202) 842-0200
website: www.cato.org
The Cato Institute is an organization of research scholars dedicated to the ideals of limited government, individual liberty, free markets, and peace. Their efforts directed at nonpartisan research and analysis are on a wide range of issues. They distribute their message through a variety of media resources and have articles about the National Popular Vote on their website.

FairVote
6930 Carroll Avenue, Suite 610
Takoma Park, MD 20912
(301) 270-4616
email: info@fairvote.org
website: www.fairvote.org
FairVote is an organization dedicated to bringing reform to American elections through access to democracy, fair representation, and fair elections. This agency works toward reforms that give all Americans greater choice, a strong voice, and a representative democracy which works for all citizens. FairVote is a trailblazer for nonpartisan change.

Federal Election Commission (FEC)
999 E Street NW
Washington, DC 20463
(800) 424-9530
website: www.fec.gov
The FEC was created to encourage participation and confidence in the democratic process in the United States. The FEC is an independent regulatory agency run by six commissioners that function in making nonpartisan decisions. This agency offers publications that explain and outline federal campaign finance laws.

Freedom Foundation
PO Box 552
Olympia, WA 98507
(360) 956-3482
email: Info@myFreedomFoundation.com
website: www.freedomfoundation.com
The Freedom Foundation is a nonprofit think tank. Their mission is to advance free enterprise, individual liberty, and accountable government. They support constitutional federalism and consequently work to inform citizens about what they consider a threat to election security, namely the National Popular Vote.

Heritage Foundation
214 Massachusetts Avenue NE
Washington, DC 20022
(202) 546-4400
email: info@heritage.org
website: www.heritage.org
The Heritage Foundation is a conservative research center and think tank dedicated to the principles of individual freedom, limited government, free enterprise, traditional American values, and a strong national defense. The policy research is shared with congressional staff members, policymakers, congressional members, news media, and the academic community.

League of Women Voters
1730 M Street NW, Suite 1000
Washington, DC 20036-4508
(202) 429-1965
website: www.lwv.org
The League of Women Voters is an organization that works to improve government and at the same time see that all citizens are active in voting. This organization pursues a vision where all Americans have a voice that they enact through voting and seeks to improve elections and educate voters.

National Conference of State Legislatures (NCSL)
444 N. Capitol Street NW, Suite 515
Washington, DC 20001
(202) 624-5400
website: www.ncsl.org
The NCSL is a bipartisan organization providing support, ideas, connections, and a strong voice on Capitol Hill for states. NCSL is a champion of state legislatures and works to promote the effectiveness of state legislatures and policy innovation and communication between state legislatures and to make certain that state legislatures have a strong voice in the federal system.

National Popular Vote (NPV)
Box 1441
Los Altos, CA 94023
(650) 472-1587
email: info@nationalpopularvote.com
website: www.nationalpopularvote.com
National Popular Vote (NPV) is a nonprofit organization working to engage states to join the coalition to enact a nationwide US popular vote for president. The NPV educates the public to promote the national popular vote as an alternative election system to replace the Electoral College.

Save Our States
1401 N. Lincoln Boulevard
Oklahoma City, OK 73104
(405) 602-1667
email: trent@saveourstates.com
website: www.saveourstates.com

Save Our States is a group of individuals who care about the United States. This group is dedicated to protecting personal freedoms by preserving constitutional federalism. They support the Electoral College, and their opinions are voiced against the National Popular Vote.

For Further Reading

Abramowitz, Alan. *Voice of the People: Elections and Voting in the United States.* New York, NY: McGraw-Hill Humanities, 2003. This book helps readers understand why American voters are disengaged with the voting process and analyzes the techniques used to research elections and voting behavior.

Archer, J. Clark. *Historical Atlas of U.S. Presidential Elections 1788-2004.* Thousand Oaks, CA: CQ Press, 2006. This book presents a historical atlas of presidential elections and analyzes patterns and trends in voting. It examines key data and results from each election.

Belenky, Alexander S. *Who Will Be the Next President?* New York, NY: Springer Verlag, 2016. This book addresses the present presidential election system and analyzes the proposed National Popular Vote plan and how it may violate the Equal Protection Clause.

Clinton, Hillary Rodham. *What Happened?* New York, NY: Simon & Schuster, 2017. This work explains the presidential election process and experience from Hillary Clinton's point of view. Clinton details her experience running as the first woman candidate from a majority party for election as president.

Hasen, Richard L. *The Voting Wars: From Florida 2000 to the Next Election Meltdown.* Cambridge, MA: Yale University Press, 2012. This work analyzes the election rules from a nonpartisan viewpoint. Hasen contends that future election disputes will be worse, amplified by social media and increasingly distorted by unsubstantiated claims.

Keyssar, Alexander. *The Right to Vote: The Contested History of Democracy in the United States.* New York/NY: Basic Books, 2009. Keyssar presents a history of voting in the United States and analyzes the relationship between social class and voter rights.

Maisel, Louis Sandy. *American Political Parties and Elections: A Very Short Introduction.* Oxford, UK: Oxford University Press, 2007. This brief history of the main political parties in the United States also analyzes the Electoral College system and its underlying flaws.

Ross, Tara. *Enlightened Democracy: The Case for the Electoral College.* Dallas, TX: Colonial Press, 2009. Ross examines the role of the Electoral College in selecting presidents and concludes that the Electoral College system protects our republic and promotes liberty.

Wang, Tova Andrea. *The Politics of Voter Suppression: Defending and Expanding Americans' Right to Vote.* Ithaca, NY: Cornell University Press, 2012. Wang analyzes how voting access has changed in the United States and argues that voter suppression tactics are typically illegitimate and partisan.

Periodicals and Internet Sources

Adler, Hank, "Breaking the Constitution-National Popular Vote Interstate Compact," Townhall, May 3, 2014. https://townhall.com/columnists/hankadler/2014/05/03/breaking-the-constitution—national-popular-vote-interstate-compact-n1832757.

Anderson, Meg, "Critics Move to Scrap the Electoral College, But It's Not Likely to Work," NPR, November 17, 2016. http://www.npr.org/2016/11/17/502292749/critics-move-to-trash-the-electoral-college-but-its-not-likely-to-work.

BBC News, "What is the US Electoral College," BBC News, August 25, 2016. http://www.bbc.com/news/world-us-canada-15764542.

Beinart, Peter, "The Electoral College Was Meant to Stop People Like Trump From Being President," *Atlantic*, November 21, 2016. https://www.theatlantic.com/politics/archive/2016/11/the-electoral-college-was-meant-to-stop-men-like-trump-from-being-president/508310/.

Cooper, Matthew, "Trump's New Favorite College," Newsweek Middle East, November 30, 2016. http://newsweekme.com/trumps-new-favorite-college/.

Gregg, Gary L, "Unpopular Vote," American Conservative, December 15, 2011. http://www.theamericanconservative.com/articles/unpopular-vote/.

Keneally, Meghan, "A Split on Popular and Electoral College Vote Not Out of the Question," ABC News, November 1, 2016. http://abcnews.go.com/Politics/split-popular-electoral-college-vote-question/story?id=43215235.

Koza, John, "The President Should be Elected by National Popular Vote," The Hill, September 12, 2016. http://thehill.com/blogs/congress-blog/presidential-campaign/295346-the-president-should-be-elected-by-national-popular.

Lepore, Jill, "How to Steal An Election," *New Yorker*, July 4, 2016. http://www.newyorker.com/magazine/2016/07/04/conventions-primaries-and-the-presidency.

Moulitsas, Markos, "Markos Moulitsas: Our Rigged System," The Hill, November 15, 2016. http://thehill.com/opinion/markos-moulitsas/306185-markos-moulitsas-our-rigged-system.

New York Times Editorial, "Drop Out of the College," *New York Times*, March 14, 2006. http://www.nytimes.com/2006/03/14/opinion/drop-out-of-the-college.html.

Robertson, Brian, and Rob Wasinger, "Every State a Swing," American Conservative, February 22, 2016. http://www.theamericanconservative.com/articles/every-state-a-swing/.

Silberstein, Steve, "How to Make the Electoral College Work for Everyone," *Washington Monthly*. http://washingtonmonthly.com/magazine/marchaprilmay-2017/how-to-make-the-electoral-college-work-for-everyone/.

Time, "These 3 Common Arguments for Preserving the Electoral College are Wrong," *Time*, November 15, 2016. http://time.com/4571626/electoral-college-wrong-arguments/.

Waldman, Michael, "Majority Rule at Last," *Washington Monthly*, April 2008. http://washingtonmonthly.com/magazine/april-2008/majority-rule-at-last/.

Weber, Sam, and Laura Fong, "This System Calls for Popular Vote to Determine Winner," *PBS NewsHour*, November 6, 2016. http://www.pbs.org/newshour/bb/proposal-calls-popular-vote-determine-winner/.

Williams, Weston, "Could 'Faithless Electors' Undermine the Electoral College?" *Christian Science Monitor*, November 22, 2016. https://www.csmonitor.com/USA/Politics/2016/1122/Could-faithless-electors-undermine-the-Electoral-College.

Websites

League of Women Voters (http://lwv.org)
This website contains information to support and encourage all citizens in the act of voting. The league helps to encourage voting on all levels.

National Popular Vote! (www.nationalpopularvote.com)
This website aims to inform and educate the public about the proposal to change the system of presidential election in the United States. Backed by National Popular Vote Inc., a nonprofit corporation, it has proposed the nationwide popular election for president.

PBS Election Central
(http://www.pbseduelectioncentral.com/election-collection)
This website provides resources to learn about presidential elections in the United States and includes information about civic engagement and democracy.

Index

of 2000, 8–9, 17, 18, 23, 28–29, 49–50, 51, 63, 78–79, 82
of 2016, 25, 39, 40, 41, 62, 66, 67–68, 73, 77–78, 79–80, 92
presidential primaries, need for reform of, 44, 100–105

R

ranked choice, 39, 43–44, 62, 65
Reagan, Ronald, 79
Richie, Rob, 86–93
Roosevelt, Theodore, 63, 79
Ross, Tara, 21–22

S

Santens, Scott, 39–45, 52
slavery, Electoral College's roots in, 9, 15–19

T

Taft, William Howard, 63, 79
Texas, 42, 51, 90, 91, 102
  discriminatory voting laws in, 18
three-fifths compromise, 15, 17, 18
Tilden, Samuel J., 27, 28
Trump, Donald, 25, 41, 43, 62, 66, 67, 68, 76, 77, 78, 79, 80, 102, 103
Twelfth Amendment, 25, 31

U

US Constitution, 7, 9, 12, 15, 16, 17, 18, 25, 26, 28, 29, 41, 51, 52, 53, 54–55, 56, 89, 91

US territories, inability to vote in US presidential elections, 59

V

voter id laws, 18
voter's illusion, 69, 72
voting, reasons why people do it, 69–74
Voting Rights Act of 1965, 18

W

Wilson, Woodrow, 63, 79
Wisconsin, 68, 77, 88
Wyoming, 34, 37, 48, 49, 51

Picture Credits

Cover txking/Shutterstock.com; p.10 Spencer Platt/Hulton Archive/ Getty Images; p. 13 Mark Wilson/Getty Images; p. 16 rdegrie/iStock/ Thinkstock; p. 21 GraphicaArtis/Archive Photos/Getty Images; p. 26 Evan El-Amin/Shutterstock.com; p. 33 Alex Wong/Getty Images; p. 38 © iStockphoto.com/shmell c4; p. 40 Win McNamee/ Getty Images; p. 47 Joseph Sohm/Shutterstock.com; p. 55 Library of Congress Prints and Photographs Division; p. 64 AFP/Getty Images; p. 71 © iStockphoto.com/cbarnesphotography; p. 75 Chip Somodevilla/Getty Images; p. 77 Bloomberg/Getty Images; p. 83 © iStockphoto.com/OlegAlbinsky; p. 88 Encyclopaedia Britannica/ Universal Images Group/Getty Images; p. 95 Jeff Topping/Getty Images; p. 101 Ted Soqui/Corbis News/Getty Images